W9-CAX-020

Unchosen

Unchosen

The Hidden Lives of Hasidic Rebels

Hella Winston

Beacon Press, Boston

Beacon Press
25 Beacon Street
Boston, Massachusetts 02108-2892
www.beacon.org

Beacon Press books
are published under the auspices of
the Unitarian Universalist Association of Congregations.

Printed in the United States of America

08 07 06 05 8 7 6 5 4 3 2

This book is printed on acid-free paper that meets the uncoated paper
ANSI/NISO specifications for permanence as revised in 1992.

Text design by Bob Kosturko
Composition by Wilsted & Taylor Publishing Services

Library of Congress Cataloging-in-Publication Data

Winston, Hella.
Unchosen : the hidden lives of Hasidic rebels / Hella Winston.—1st ed.
p. cm.
Includes bibliographical references.
ISBN 0-8070-3626-9 (cloth : alk. paper) 1. Jews—New York (State)—
New York—Biography. 2. Hasidim—New York (State)—New York—
Biography. 3. Hasidim—New York (State)—New York—Social conditions.
4. New York (N.Y.)—Religion. I. Title.
F128.9.J5W55 2005
305.6'968332'097471—dc22
2005007929

In memory of my grandparents,
Salamon and Hella Schönberg

Contents

The nature of the subject matter of this book required me to change the names and certain aspects of the characters who appear on its pages, with the exception of Malkie Schwartz, whose name is her own. In some cases, elements of particular events were changed as well. These changes were made solely to protect the privacy of those who, in many cases, took serious risks to share their stories. These changes, however, do not alter the essential truth of their experiences, or of their thoughts and feelings about those experiences.

Introduction

As I glance around the large dining room table, I am struck by just how oddly familiar these women seem to me, although I have never actually met any of them before. They are all members of the extremely insular Satmar Hasidic sect. Socializing with a secular Jew like me—let alone having one in their home for a meal—is something most would do only under very unusual circumstances, if at all. The women are all dressed modestly, in long skirts, thick stockings, high-necked sweaters, and monochromatic cloth turbans that expose no hair. But, despite their dress, and their frequent lapses into Yiddish I can only intermittently understand, there is something about these Satmar women that reminds me of some of the women in my extended family, even several of my friends. Is it in their features, I wonder? There is, after all, great variety here: a few have dark eyes and olive skin, while others are fairer, with freckles, or blue eyes. Perhaps it's something less tangible or purely physical—like the forceful, animated way they are speaking over one another, or their constant concern that I have enough food on my plate.

Whatever it is, I do know that after so many frustrating weeks of trying to find a way into this community for my doctoral dissertation in sociology, I am excited, and more than a little nervous, to be sitting here. Of course, I was prepared for how difficult gaining access would be, given what I had read and heard about how fervently the Satmarers seek to avoid contact with outsiders. If I wanted to meet Hasidic people, I was told repeatedly, I should go to Crown Heights. There, Lubavitchers zealously court the opportunity to introduce unaffiliated Jews to the beauty of "true" Judaism.

Indeed, a good many popular accounts of Hasidic Jews have focused on Lubavitch. Several Jewish journalists and scholars have produced largely admiring books describing the compelling Lubavitch philosophy, way of life, and formidable outreach efforts.[1] With its "*mitzvah* tanks," campus *Chabad* houses, celebrity-studded fundraising telethons, and outposts across the globe, Lubavitch has become almost synonymous with Hasidism. This despite the fact that in the United States it numbers less than half the size of Satmar[2] and is hardly representative of the Hasidic community as a whole. With their mission—unique in the Hasidic world—to attract unaffiliated Jews, Lubavitchers are raised to engage with (Jewish) outsiders, doing missionary work wherever Jews are found around the world.[3] As Sue Fishkoff[4] so vividly documents, however, Lubavitch missionaries do this apparently without compromising their strictly Orthodox way of life.

This emphasis on proselytizing has meant that a significant percentage of Lubavitchers were not born into the community, but joined by choice. Often those who join, known as *baalei teshuvah* ("masters of return"), have led formerly secular (or at least non-Orthodox) lives, which likely included a college education or beyond. In fact, in her book on Lubavitch girls, Stephanie Wellin-Levine asserts that in the year 2000, 70 percent of the Lubavitch girls' school's graduating class came from baalei teshuvah homes.[5] This focus on proselytizing has, understandably, fueled much of the interest in this group.[6] Additionally, Lubavitch raises a substantial amount of money from non-Hasidic Jews,[7]—including Revlon billionaire Ronald Perelman and cosmetics mogul Ronald Lauder—who apparently support its mission without any intention of committing to the lifestyle. All of this is in strong contrast to the other Hasidic sects, which include Satmar, Ger, Viznitz, Belz, Bobov, Skver, Spinka, Pupa, and Breslov, to name only a few. In these sects, almost all members are born into the community, and none engages in formal outreach, making them comparatively more insulated from, and less aware of, the ways of the outside society than their counterparts in Lubavitch.

It was precisely for these reasons that I did not want to go to Crown Heights. While Lubavitch's openness to even the most secular Jew would have made gaining access to that community fairly easy, it was, to a great extent, the self-imposed insularity and segregation of the Hasidim that had made me so interested in them to begin with. Also, given that so many Lubavitchers join that community by choice, I felt that any in-depth inquiry into the daily life of Lubavitch would require both an exploration of the motivations and experiences of such people, and a consideration of the effect of this phenomenon on the group as a whole—tasks I was not prepared to undertake. Further, I was concerned that the Lubavitch interest in and skill at proselytizing—not to mention its apparently sophisticated PR operation—might actually make it *more* difficult for me to get a complete picture of what everyday life was like in that community. Groups that are trying to attract potential members, even those with the purest of intentions, are not apt to expose such people to anything that might undermine this goal.

As a result, I decided I would try to find a way into one of the other communities, and it was ultimately through a doctor friend in Brooklyn with a large Hasidic practice that I made contact with Suri, a Satmar woman and my hostess for this evening. When the doctor first agreed to tell Suri about my interest in meeting Hasidic people, and to give her my telephone number, I hadn't actually expected her to call. After all, Satmar is considered to be the most insular and right-wing of all the Hasidic sects, and anti-Zionist to boot.[8] But, to my surprise, Suri did call, and our first conversation over the phone lasted close to an hour. Before we hung up, Suri told me that she would like to have me to her Brooklyn home for dinner. She wanted me to meet some of her closest friends—all women deeply involved in the life of their community.[9] I felt as if I had struck gold.

I was impressed, during that initial call, by Suri's apparent warmth and openness, her sense of humor and sophistication. She seemed to have traveled widely, and she held a demanding job in the community—something that, while by no means unheard of, is still not the norm for Hasidic women, given their tremendous responsibilities for childcare and the home.[10] I was also touched that Suri wanted to arrange such a dinner for my benefit. From talking to her, I had the sense that she had decided to speak with me mainly out of a feeling of gratitude toward the doctor who had put us in touch; her husband had been seriously ill, and Suri told me that she believed that the doctor—as God's messenger—had saved his life. I supposed that having me to her home and answering my questions was the least Suri felt she could do in return for her husband's good health. Of course, some people had also told me that Suri would likely consider it a mitzvah, or an act of kindness and religious obligation, to expose me to the beauty of Judaism and the Hasidic way of life.

But it felt as if Suri and I had responded to one another on a more personal level as well. My mother is a Holocaust survivor. Her parents were murdered in Auschwitz. For the duration of the war, she and her sister were hidden by a Protestant family in the countryside of their native Hungary. The Satmar sect originated in Hungary as well, and the Satmar community in America was built mostly by Hungarian refugees from World War II. Although, to the best of anyone's knowledge, none of my mother's relatives had been Hasidic, the fact that we were *landsmen* seemed to appeal to Suri. And despite my fears, she did not seem at all judgmental about my total lack of religious observance.

If I was pleasantly surprised by Suri's openness to me, whatever the reason, it was all the more striking in light of the far from neutral reactions I had begun to get from friends and acquaintances when they learned of my plans to do research among the Hasidim. While many of my non-Jewish friends seemed to express a kind of anthropological curiosity about the project, intrigued by the prospect of my getting to hang out with such apparently holy, albeit odd-looking, people ("Aren't they like the Amish, medieval and totally against technology?" they would invariably ask me, betraying serious misunderstanding), the Jewish ones were a different story altogether.

Some revealed a kind of admiration for the Hasidim, believing them to be the only bulwark against the extinction of an "authentic," imperiled Judaism that nobody else—themselves included—had the dedication to uphold. And then there were those for whom the Hasidic way of life—or, more accurately, what they perceived that life to be—evoked a kind of romantic longing, bolstered by a sense that these communities represented an attractive response to the shallowness and anomie characteristic of contemporary life. Others could not see why on earth I would want to spend time among such people. After all, weren't they all primitive and backward—even dirty, with those unkempt beards—an embarrassment to rational Jews everywhere? Sometimes both reactions would come from the same person, which was especially disconcerting.

Perhaps the most unexpected reaction (although I know better now) came from a modern Orthodox friend. He told me that, as a religious Jew and a Zionist, he felt no identification with the Hasidim at all—not with their withdrawal from the larger world, not with their use of Yiddish, not even with their devotion to religious study, despite his own love of learning Talmud. To his mind, Yiddish is a language of the Diaspora. It is the linguistic marker of a community in exile and, as such, is not something to be celebrated or even preserved. As long as Jews spoke Yiddish, he told me, they were perpetuating their own ghettoization. "I would rather see those guys go become cops in Tel Aviv," he declared, referring to the Hasidim, "than sit and learn all day in Williamsburg." I had begun to wonder whether the Hasidim themselves had any idea that they were a screen onto which so much Jewish ambivalence was projected.

As we start to eat, the women begin to pepper me with questions: What do I really find so interesting about them, and why would I want to spend time writing about their lives? What exactly is a dissertation, and a Ph.D., for that matter? Is there any money in this line of work? Will I publish a book, and will they be in it? Will they become famous?

Despite their enviable poise and composure—the room is quite warm, and I know I'd be perspiring heavily under that much clothing—these women are hardly meek or shy, as those who would equate a tradition-bound role with submissiveness might expect. Their profound lack of familiarity with the ways of the outside culture is striking, certainly. Contemporary Hasidic ideology dictates that they be raised to avoid almost all exposure to what the community understands to be the corrupt secular society, which means that these women (along with their male counterparts) are not supposed to watch television, see movies, read secular books or newspapers, listen to secular music, follow sports, use the Internet (except for business), or attend college. This does not stop them from being curious, however, and from trying to get a clear picture of who I am and what it is I want from them.

I try to explain as best I can that I am interested in them because, even though, of course, we are all Jewish, their lives are so different from mine. I say this fully aware, however, that, for these women, "Jewish" is synonymous with Hasidic, or at least Orthodox, and that, to them, all other Jews are in some sense not really Jewish. I also tell them that it seems to me that their lives must be quite challenging. Responsible for bearing and raising as many children as possible to husbands they have met only once or twice before marriage, they are expected to focus on maintaining a Jewish home and family. Indeed, this responsibility for the family and home exempts women from engaging in the "time bound" commandments that men are obligated to perform, and also from undertaking the rigorous religious study men are commanded to pursue. In fact, women are considered not to have the "proper mind" for such study. How do they handle so many children, I ask. Do they ever get time for themselves? Do they sometimes wish they could sit and learn as the men do?

The women immediately jump in to correct my misimpression. They know all about feminism, they say, but the feminists are wrong. They are happy and fulfilled by what they do—bringing Jewish children into the world and raising them in a Jewish home and community is the most important work there is. And the men certainly don't have it so easy themselves, being obligated to study, as well as pray three times a day. Yes, of course Hasidic women have their challenges. This life is not always easy—on the body or the spirit—but, then again, it is hard to be a Jew, and we all must make sacrifices to live as God's chosen. Their way is to seek constantly to improve themselves and their understanding, and to know that God has His reasons for creating the challenges they face.

Getting an education and going to college might be perfectly all right for non-Jews, but for Hasidic people it is irrelevant, the women explain. They learn all they need to know within the community, which, by being good wives and mothers, they are helping to perpetuate. They are also doing this through their tremendous involvement in community charity. Some Hasidic women even work for pay, helping to support their families as teachers or administrators in the schools, or in other organizations or businesses that serve the community or are run by Hasidim. Further, because Hasidic women focus not on the theoretical aspects of Jewish law, but on its practical, everyday applications, most of them actually learn to speak and read better in English, and know more math, than the men. In school, boys devote only a small portion of their time to these subjects. Ironically, women's exemption from religious study generally results in their being much more competent than their male counterparts to interact with the outside world, when such interaction is necessary.

As I listen, I try to imagine myself in their place. This is impossible, of course. There is no way I can erase the effects of my upbringing and education, all of my prior socialization and ways of thinking about life and the world. But is it even accurate, or intellectually honest, for me to assume that if these women had been raised as I had, they would automatically feel as I do: namely, that their way of life is ultimately too narrow and oppressive, too intolerant of dissent and difference—despite its potentially compelling emphasis on family and community (apparently, even over material wealth) and its commitment to the maintenance of tradition and a connection to the past? Surely, these women would argue that I simply lack the proper understanding. They would claim that my failure to acknowledge and accept the true and eternal nature of the Torah prevents me from seeing through the obvious—though seductive—lies and distortions of modernity. If I only understood this basic truth, they might tell me, I would embrace their way of life.

Does it finally come down to a question of faith, then? Of what each of us believes about God, if we believe in God to begin with? Do these women choose and find contentment with this life because, fundamentally, they believe? I have to assume they do, and, suddenly, I am able to make more sense of the scene around the table. To have such faith, and to live in accordance with it, can be both beautiful and humbling, and I cannot help but find myself respecting these women for that. I may not be able to muster their conviction, or to reconcile what they believe with other things I know about the world and how it works, but I want and need them to help me see it from their perspective.

It is getting late, and, one by one, the women excuse themselves, citing children who need bathing and bedtime stories. Several mention that it is very rare for them to have a night out like this, an occasion to reflect on and talk about their lives. One woman who was relatively quiet throughout the evening explains that the religion's emphasis on female modesty sometimes makes her feel that women should resist talking about themselves at all. Some scribble their phone numbers in my notebook and let me know that I can call them again for a more personal interview. Others say they would like to invite me to a *Shabbos* meal.

The guests have all left, and Suri motions for me to sit down. I do, and she pulls her chair next to mine. "So, what did you think?" she asks, somewhat conspiratorially.

Just then, Suri's daughter, Chanie, arrives at the apartment. Chanie introduces herself to me and smiles. "So, what did you think?" she asks, echoing her mother's words and tone precisely. She has a mischievous glint in her eye. It's then I notice that Chanie, in contrast to the other women, is wearing a very pretty light brown wig (no turban) and a fashionable suede skirt and matching top.

I tell Chanie and Suri that I found the women impressive—spirited and self-confident, despite their obvious modesty. I say that I am eager to spend more time among them, learning about how they negotiate the responsibilities of their demanding lives. Chanie smiles politely, waits a minute, then replies, "Well, that's all very well and good, but do you want to hear the real story, the truth?" I hesitate, unsure of what to say. "The truth?" she asks again, her eyebrows raised with intent. I am stunned and still say nothing.

Chanie makes it clear to me that she is profoundly religious, that she loves Judaism and the Hasidic way of life. She and her husband keep all the commandments, and they are raising their daughter to do the same. But then she looks at her mother and says, "I bet they talked all about their children and how wonderful their lives are, didn't they?" Her mother nods and suppresses a laugh.

"These women are very secretive," Chanie declares. "Look, there is negativity and then there is the truth. And the truth includes positive *and* negative." Yes, they may seem confident, she concedes, but that's because most of them haven't been exposed to different points of view enough to have their confidence challenged. "These women are not able to be honest, especially in a group," Chanie continues. "There is a lot of hypocrisy here among the Satmar women, and a high rate of suicide. They don't know how to go any deeper than their shirt. They may know the truth subconsciously, but they are not even aware of it."

I don't know how to respond. I might not have been startled to hear comments like this from someone outside of the Hasidic community, but from a devout Hasidic woman? I also wonder: Is this true about the suicide rate? I have spoken to a variety of doctors and therapists who treat Hasidic patients, and many have remarked on the prevalence of anxiety and depressive disorders among the Hasidim in general. Some have attributed this, in part, to the complex legacy of the Holocaust. But suicide? I haven't heard or seen any information on that. If Chanie's comment is true, it is certainly news to me. If it's not, I wonder whether this is her way of trying to communicate something about the degree of unhappiness she, or some of the other women she may know, might have experienced. Whatever the reality, the comment is striking in and of itself.

"No one will ever say that their kid drove them crazy, because that would imply that they are not good mothers," Chanie continues. "And there is a lot of emphasis on appearance. The women are formal and neat and put together, but not chic, and do not express any individuality. And everyone monitors everyone else."

Suri agrees, and notes that when people come over to her home, she has to put away all of the photographs of Chanie's wedding that show her hand on her husband's shoulder. This is a gesture of affection considered inappropriately intimate by community standards. She also has to hide the books she reads in English (the language of the corrupt outside culture)—not just novels, but books about psychology or health—for fear that the women will talk about her as being "too modern." Such a designation could shatter her unmarried children's marriage (and possibly even job) prospects, as too much contact with the outside world is perceived by most as evidence of irredeemable moral corruption.

With marriages arranged by a matchmaker, whose job requires that he or she gather detailed information about both parties, guarding one's reputation is essential. Despite the Jewish prohibition against gossip, or *lashon hara*, in practice, Hasidic communities depend on it for their survival and perpetuation: marriage is the main engine of community reproduction, and everybody wants to secure a good match.

"And I still don't understand why I can't drive, why it's considered immodest," Suri says with a shrug. "But that's what we believe. That's how it goes here, by us."

Suri thinks that she is "corrupt," possibly because her early youth on the Lower East Side was freer and more open than the community allows today (her father read the *New York Times* and *U.S. News and World Report* at home). Unlike the majority of Hasidim, who arrived after the war, her parents were not recent immigrants, refugees from Hitler, but "Yankees" whose families had been in this country since the late nineteenth century. Although they were religiously observant, they were also on the well-trodden path of assimilation. Her mother was a "real New York lady," who, as a younger woman, had devoured mystery novels and loved nothing more than dressing up for an evening out at Radio City Music Hall.

Indeed, for someone like Suri, the growing insularity of the Hasidic community has been hard to fully understand. Like most, however, she has accepted it. It's just that, born in New York, Suri was raised to be an American. She was brought up listening to the president's speeches on the radio, and taught to smile at the mailman and exchange greetings with the neighbors and local merchants, whether they were Jewish or not. Today, many people in Suri's community look askance at her for doing these things, although her basic sense of politeness prevents that from stopping her.

Nonetheless, Suri supposes that her own experience growing up made her a bit more lenient with her children than she should have been. She also notes that, because her husband's illness prevented the couple from having more than three children (two boys and a girl), her family has always been different; most have seven or eight children, if not more. As it is, Chanie has to hide from all of her friends that she goes to the public library and takes out five books a week, or sometimes even visits the Metropolitan Museum. Viewing graven images—not to mention the Christian iconography and nudity on display in all of that painting and sculpture—is considered by some of the more extreme members of her community to be particularly corrupting. If people knew that Chanie did these things, or that she often rented a bike and rode it, wearing a skirt, around Central Park, she could lose her teaching job in the community: the powers that be would likely perceive her as a potential danger to young girls' developing minds. But these activities are important to Chanie, and she and her fortunately open-minded husband don't believe that they undermine her religious commitment in any way. Just to be safe, however, they don't dare share this information with any of their acquaintances.

Chanie then tells me that she feels that she had her baby too young (at nineteen) and was robbed of her youth. She loves her daughter, of course, but sometimes she still resents having had a child so early. Of course, she could have opted to wait another year or so. It was just that the peer and community pressure had been so great. In the community, if a woman isn't nursing a baby within a year of her wedding, people begin to talk, theorizing about what might be wrong with her, and offering their pity.

"And did you notice all of their '*Baruch Hashems*'?" Suri interrupts.

I had noticed them, though I was prepared; Hasidic people often say "Baruch Hashem," or "Thank God," after they are asked how they are, or, indeed, whenever they refer to anything positive in their lives. This functions as a kind of hedge against the evil eye.

"I have a real problem with that. If something is not going well, I admit it. I am honest," Suri declares.

Indeed. My head is spinning. An hour ago, I convinced myself that I would endeavor to see the lives of these women *from their own perspectives*, which, all in all, appeared to be quite positive. I was going to enlist them in helping me to understand and try to convey the richness of meaning with which they endowed their day-to-day existence. But here is another perspective entirely, and I suspect that, while it might be less typical—or at least less openly articulated—it is no less important.

In one sense, the fact that some Hasidic people might express discontent, or break rules and transgress their community's symbolic boundaries, should not come as a tremendous surprise. In any society, there is always a gap between ideology and the complicated reality of lived experience, where individual expression almost always finds a way of asserting itself within and against even the most rigid of social structures. Indeed, it is possible that Suri's willingness to speak with me in the first place represented just such an act of self-expression. This was a chance to tell her thoughts to a presumably neutral outsider who would not hold her to the standards of her community and with whom she might also test and even alter her views about the outside world. Nonetheless, it was still startling to hear her comments.

Why? For one thing, nothing in the scholarly literature had quite prepared me for Suri and Chanie's candor, or for the views they were expressing (although the film *A Price Above Rubies* and the novel *The Romance Reader*, both fictional accounts of Hasidic women at odds with their communities, had made me curious). While the scholarly literature does contain some discussion of Hasidic discontent and transgression, it is fairly limited. Further, this work tends to attribute their occurrence primarily to problems of individual adjustment, or to a breakdown in the community's ability to control its members. Neither view seems to give much weight to the subjective experiences and interpretations of Hasidic people themselves.[11] Suri and Chanie's comments made me wonder whether such views and behaviors might be more widespread than anyone had assumed or wanted to reveal, particularly because doing so might be perceived as an airing of Jewish dirty laundry, reflecting badly on the Jews as a whole—something of a Jewish preoccupation.

Of course, there is also no doubt that it is much more appealing to believe that all of the people who are living this life are doing so because they believe in it, freely, by choice, and without questions or doubts; that everyone in these communities is unwaveringly pious, living in a constant state of religious ecstasy; that structuring one's life around devotion to God and His eternal, unchanging Torah somehow grants one immunity from the trials of being a human being in a specific time and place.

But I also had to admit that the more I heard from Suri and Chanie, the more unsettled I became. It was difficult to learn from actual people—more even than from books or articles or films—about how restrictive this life could be, and what a toll that could take on those living it. Indeed, it was hard for me to reconcile this idea of Judaism with what I had always admired about the tradition—namely, its profound insights into human psychology and social life, its wisdom about how to treat others and behave in the world. And I also found it hard to square what I was hearing about Hasidic life with Hasidism's particular emphasis on mysticism, egalitarianism, and joyful devotion to God, even over the rigid adherence to the law that characterizes some other forms of Judaism. Although, intellectually, I understood the Hasidic community's religious and sociological reasons for these restrictions, it was still hard for me to fathom that there really could be Jewish people, indeed entire Jewish communities, who actually believed that reading books or viewing art or having a profession could be a *bad*, even dangerous, thing. And it was disquieting to see what a big role fear and shame seemed to play in enforcing these values.

Didn't Jews thrive on open discussion and debate? Indeed, wasn't debate at the very heart of the tradition? Didn't Jews also value education and ideas, pride themselves on producing and consuming culture? Not just contemporary secular Jews, of course, but Jews throughout history? In fact, wasn't it the great Jewish thinker Maimonides who, in the Middle Ages, strove to reconcile the philosophy and science of Aristotle with the Bible, engaging the writings of Arab Muslim philosophers? And he did all of this while also working as a physician! And today, these young Hasidim were not even allowed to read Aristotle, let alone go to college or medical school—or to the movies, or even to a Broadway musical, like *Fiddler on the Roof*. After all, this was a community that prohibited men from hearing women sing because the sound of their voices could be sexually arousing. How did it come to this?

As I walked through the bustling Williamsburg streets back to the subway that night, I was overwhelmed with questions; indeed, it would take many months before I could even begin to make sense of what I had experienced at Suri's home. I knew that there was something I liked about Suri and Chanie. I found things to admire about the other women as well, despite their possible burnishing of the truth of their lives; after all, who among us is always honest with herself and with others about the true nature of her experiences?

But mostly that evening I was left wondering if there were more women—and men, for that matter—like Suri and Chanie in these communities. Were there others who were indulging their individual needs and desires in secret, forced, out of fear of community censure or worse, to conceal their thoughts and activities from their neighbors, friends, and relatives? I wanted to know if there were more people who felt stifled by the conformity and the secrecy, who were longing to engage with the outside culture and the wider world. Might some people be even *less* sanguine than Suri and her daughter, those who were unable or unwilling to sneak around or keep up appearances?

I knew that in order to investigate the answers to these questions, I would need to meet and get to know others who would be willing to let me into their lives and involve me in some of their most intimate thoughts and conversations.

Since that dinner, almost two years ago, I have spent many hundreds of hours among people like Suri and Chanie: Hasidim from a wide variety of sects—including, as it would turn out, even Lubavitch—who, despite an attachment to the religion and to certain elements of Hasidic culture, also feel oppressed by their community's rigid rules, behavioral restrictions, and social scrutiny. As a result, such people find themselves leading all manner of double lives in order to pursue their desires. These can include anything from seeing movies, listening to jazz, and reading philosophy, to finding intimacy with someone from outside the community. I have also met those who no longer believe but nonetheless feel they must remain in the community.

Some of these people are able to cope fairly easily with the compartmentalization required of such a life. Others suffer terribly, and often alone, not wanting to live as hypocrites, but also knowing that making the decision to abandon the community's way of life would likely come at a huge personal cost: possible rejection by their families and community, guilt about bringing shame on their relatives and abandoning their traditions, and tremendous anxiety about the difficulty of making a life in a lonely and unfamiliar outside world.

I have met others who—for reasons ranging from an intense desire for greater personal or intellectual freedom, to religious doubts, to the need to escape physical or sexual abuse—found it impossible to remain within this social structure. These people have taken the terrifying step of leaving the community, and sometimes the religion, altogether.

In order to meet and get to know these people—close to sixty in all—I spent time in places ranging from a dilapidated walk-up apartment on the outskirts of a Hasidic neighborhood in Brooklyn that functioned as a hangout for Hasidic "misfits," to the secluded nooks of the library of the Jewish Theological Seminary, whose non-Hasidic books make it forbidden territory. Along the way, and when possible, I visited with people in their homes, both within and outside of various Hasidic communities. Starbucks was also a frequent haunt, a meeting place of choice for many Hasidim still living within their communities. I also logged countless hours in the virtual spaces of the Internet, where people are able to take advantage of the anonymity of cyberspace to express themselves and try to connect with, and gain support from, others in similar situations.

In addition to conducting one-on-one interviews, I also participated in a variety of social events, both within Hasidic communities and outside of them. I attended lectures and teas with Hasidic women and holiday celebrations in Hasidic homes. I also went to movies, concerts, parties, and other social gatherings with men and women who have left, or are in the process of leaving, these communities.

The stories that appear in this book are those of individual people and, in one case, a composite of several. While constraints on space and time of course prohibit recounting the stories of everyone I met, those that follow are generally representative of what I learned from and experienced among those who became a part of this research.

It is impossible to get an accurate sense of the number of Hasidic people who are transgressing against or struggling to leave their communities. For obvious reasons, such people don't advertise themselves. Further, because the Hasidim choose not to maintain a census, reliable statistics that might indicate something about community attrition are not readily available. However, my experience meeting people—whether through word of mouth, my own detective work, or simply odd luck—indicates that this phenomenon might well be quite widespread. Indeed, as word of my research spread, some people actually sought me out for interviews.

Further, a very new organization, Footsteps,[12] founded to help those who are trying to explore the world beyond their ultra-Orthodox communities, seems to be attracting a steady stream of clients. To date, about two hundred people have contacted Footsteps looking for help, with an average of five new inquiries a week. Many of these people might never have decided to take this step without the support and resources Footsteps offers. Footsteps' founder and some of its clients have been a very important part of this research.

It is necessary to note here that the term "Hasidic community" is used throughout this book to refer generally to those groups that identify themselves as Hasidic. However, there are actually many different Hasidic sects, and they do not constitute one monolithic community. All of these groups share roots in eighteenth-century Central and Eastern Europe, where Hasidism began. As the movement's original founder, the Ba'al Shem Tov, gained adherents, his disciples founded different sects throughout the region. The charismatic leaders of these sects, known as *rebbes,* developed their own particular worldviews over time. For example, Lubavitch, which originated in Russia, is considered to have a particularly cerebral philosophy, or *chassidus*. The strains of Hasidism that developed in the southern regions of this area, however, either emphasized humanistic concerns or focused primarily on miracles.[13] The various sects also differed in terms of sartorial conventions and the dialects of Yiddish they spoke.

While these differences still manifest themselves to some degree within the Hasidic world today, the myriad sects nonetheless have a tremendous amount in common—namely, their strict adherence to Jewish law and the lifestyle this promotes, as well as their separation from the outside society. For this reason, the term "Hasidic community" is used here to refer to those groups that share a common point of origin and a current set of general characteristics. Further, while Hasidic Jews form communities of belief and practice, because most tend to live in specific geographical areas, they also form communities in space as well. Throughout this book, the word "community" is used in both senses, the meaning of which should be clear from the context.

Although the nature of my inquiry required that I focus most of my attention on those Hasidim who are in some way dissatisfied with their lives in the community, I also spent time among many Hasidic people who expressed no such feelings whatsoever. I came in contact with many people who reported a high degree of spiritual, emotional, and social contentedness with their lives. Further, not surprisingly, even those I met who are struggling to live in or to leave these communities expressed positive feelings about certain aspects of the Hasidic way of life. However, the fact that those who are disaffected may constitute a minority of the Hasidic population is not, in my view, a valid reason to neglect their experiences or dismiss them as unworthy of our attention. In addition to their intrinsic interest, the lives of those on the margins of a community—what motivates them, how they are regarded and treated by the larger community, and how they, in turn, react to that treatment—also serve to reveal something about the mainstream.

It is clearly beyond the scope of this work to determine the pervasiveness of Hasidic discontent or transgression, in all of their various manifestations—the ultimate expression of which might be the decision to leave the community altogether. Rather, its primary aim remains to render this phenomenon in its specificity and nuance, giving voice to those who have largely been left out of the literature until now. And while these are, fundamentally, the stories of individuals, they combine to tell a much larger story about one group's response to its own often devastating history, and the implications of that response in the face of its people's encounter with America.

Chapter One

Changing Trains

When he heard what Yossi wanted, the barber appeared stunned at first, and then relaxed into laughter, assuming it must be some kind of joke. Yossi's left leg began to twitch as he shifted uncomfortably in the sticky leather chair. Hours earlier, he had made the decision to shave off his beard and get rid of his *peyos* for good, and if this man wasn't going to help him do it, he would find someone else who would. His whole family, except for his sixteen-year-old sister, Chayla, had just left to spend the rest of the summer at a bungalow colony in the mountains. If Yossi was really going to make the break he had been considering for so long, their vacation was his window of opportunity.

Still somewhat bemused, the barber prepared to oblige, removing his scissors and razor from the container of disinfectant. Within minutes, the beard was gone, the side curls reduced to so many dark semicircles on the barbershop floor. Taking off his black velvet *kippah*, Yossi stared at himself in the mirror and couldn't *stop* staring—in the glass panes of store windows, in the side-view mirrors of parked cars and vans, in the plastic walls of the bus shelters that lined his path to the subway stop. He was in seventh heaven. It was the greatest feeling in the world.

Yossi's plan was to head to the Upper West Side of Manhattan, to a party hosted by one of a group of secular Yiddishists he had sought out and come to know in recent months. These were people who had devoted themselves to preserving the Yiddish language, and Yossi pursued them not only because he was a huge fan of Yiddish literature, but because he figured they would find him interesting. After all, he was "the real deal," a native Yiddish speaker who had grown up Hasidic in the heart of one of the few remaining Yiddish-based cultures in the world. He also felt they would accept him since, despite his religious garb—which he had continued to wear so as not to make trouble for himself in the community—he had secretly given up being observant many months ago.

Yossi was confident that these Yiddishists would sympathize with his plight. After all, some of the older ones had come from —and left—religious backgrounds themselves. Perhaps they would prove a strong source of support, a bridge out of his community into the secular world. Maybe one of them would even offer him some sort of job and a place to stay while he figured out what to do next. As it was, Yossi lacked the skills and credentials to get a decent-paying job outside the Hasidic community.

Like all of the boys he had grown up with, Yossi had stopped studying English and math sometime around the fourth grade. Fortunately, however, his parents spoke a little English at home, so he was more fluent in the language than most of his friends. A lot of them knew only the "basic survival words, like Metro Card and Medicaid," as Yossi put it. Further, although he had spent time learning in a *kollel*, a center for advanced Torah studies, after high school, Yossi didn't have anything that could pass for a legitimate high-school diploma, or a college degree. Given his lack of credentials, applying to a secular college would be tricky. He had heard that some *yeshivas* would give or sell students a transcript filled with classes they had never taken, like Physics and History. This gave him a huge laugh. In his most desperate moments, it also gave him some hope.

On his way up to the party, Yossi decided to stop off in Greenwich Village. This was a neighborhood—like the Haight in San Francisco and the Lower East Side of Manhattan—that he wished he had been alive to experience in its heyday. With a few of his remaining dollars, he bought a bag of potato chips and a liter of Hawaiian Punch, and then planted himself on a bench in Washington Square

Park. He surveyed the early afternoon scene: summery women in decidedly immodest tank tops, people sipping coffee from thermoses as they walked their dogs, a small crowd dancing to the underwater sound of a large steel drum played by a handsome, dreadlocked black man.

If only these people in the park knew what he had looked like just hours before, Yossi thought, cracking a smile. If only his friends and family could see him sitting here now! Most of them would probably be upset and confused, some even frightened, convinced that he had completely lost his mind. His father, he knew, would be apoplectic. To his mind, a boy like Yossi had no business being in such a place, mixing freely among the goyim, who indulged their every desire "like animals," filling their "empty" lives with sex and drugs and God knows what other abominations.

Yossi had endured his father's tirades many times, but he could never bring himself to feel the way the older man did. For, while his father seemed to take great pleasure and pride in being a member of the community, finding security and even status in the insular and highly circumscribed way of life it promoted, Yossi had always chafed at the community's narrowness and rigidity. He also marveled at its uncanny ability to take aspects of religious observance that could be joyful and turn them into onerous obligations or, worse, instruments of fear—both of God and of other people. Indeed, Yossi was more afraid of the spies and tattletales in his own community than he could ever imagine being of God, if there even was a God.

Yossi felt that this was particularly ironic, given that the Ba'al Shem Tov, an eighteenth-century storyteller and folk healer in Central Europe (also known as the Besht), founded the Hasidic movement as a reaction against what he perceived to be the overly hierarchical, rigid, and legalistic Judaism of his day. Drawing on sophisticated Jewish mystical (Kabbalistic) teachings, the Besht based his movement on two theoretical concepts: religious pantheism, or the omnipresence of God, and the communion between God and man. In this view, God is present everywhere, not just in the spiritual realm but in the material world as well, and, while He surely influences the behavior of human beings, by focusing their thoughts, actions, and utterances on Him, human beings can also influence God.

According to the Besht, the righteous man is one who is in constant communion with God, even in his worldly affairs, as God is present in the material world. The Besht taught that this communion was best achieved through fervent prayer, as well as heartfelt and joyous song and dance; for him, then, the essence of religion rested in sentiment rather than reason. Therefore, he placed ecstatic prayer even above Talmudic study, which he felt was useful only when it served to produce an exalted religious mood.

By elevating these modes of worship to the level of Torah study, the Besht radically democratized worship, making authentic spirituality accessible to even the commonest Jew. While Yossi knew that there were some particularly learned Hasidim who talked and even wrote about reforming present-day Hasidic life by bringing the community back to the movement's radical roots, they tended to circulate their ideas only among themselves. And so, such notions never filtered down to the masses. Despite some of the distinctive social and cultural practices that had endured, Yossi doubted that the Ba'al Shem Tov would recognize what his movement had become.

Yossi believed that the main reason he and his father didn't see eye to eye on the community had to do with the fact that they had been raised under vastly different circumstances. Yossi's father was born in Boro Park to American-born, nominally Orthodox parents typical of their generation. Descended from Hasidim in Europe, their own parents had come to the United States seeking a better life and had raised their children to be a part of the American mainstream. Both of Yossi's grandparents had attended public high schools (his grandmother's best friend was a Catholic girl) and, though they studied Jewish subjects after school, both also ultimately went on to college. The two met at a wedding and courted openly for six months, visiting restaurants and attending plays and movies together. They married in 1948. At the time, Boro Park was a fairly prosperous community, made up of Irish and Italian families, as well as a largely American-born Jewish population.[1]

In those days, Yossi's grandmother didn't cover her hair, and, like all of her Jewish friends, she wore clothes that reflected the prevailing styles. For his part, Yossi's grandfather went around clean-shaven, wearing a suit and tie and hat, the same outfit he wore to *shul*, or synagogue, on Shabbos. The family owned a television set and, in addition to Rosh Hashanah, Yom Kippur, and Pesach, come November they also celebrated Thanksgiving, with a turkey and all the trimmings. Yossi's grandfather always insisted on that.

But then, in the mid-1960s, the neighborhood began to change.[2] Hasidim who had been living in Williamsburg and Crown Heights began moving in. Most of them were refugees from Hitler who had arrived in the United States en masse after the war. They had settled in these other Brooklyn neighborhoods under the leadership of a handful of charismatic rebbes, or spiritual leaders, who themselves had either escaped the Nazis or survived the camps. Deeply traumatized by their wartime experiences, and mostly poor and with almost no knowledge of English and the American way of life, these newly arrived Hasidim had immediately set about recreating the world that had existed for them in Europe before the Holocaust. Many considered this an obligation to those who had been murdered. It was also a clear affirmation of their refusal to be annihilated.

One of the most powerful motivations these Hasidim had for recreating their former way of life had to do with several rebbes' claims about the causes of the Holocaust. The sixth Lubavitcher rebbe taught his followers that the Holocaust was God's punishment for Jewish assimilation in Europe, and even attributed his own rescue from the Nazis to his keeping of the commandments.[3] The Satmar rebbe blamed the Holocaust on the Zionists, claiming that, according to the Torah, only the Messiah could bring Jews back to the land of Israel. To him, Zionism represented a blasphemous usurpation of God's prerogative, and was a direct cause of the slaughter of six million Jews.[4] Both taught that only the strictest adherence to a "Torah life" could protect their followers from another such horror.[5]

As a result, codes of modesty that had, for the most part, been discarded by Orthodox Jews in America were reinstated in these communities.[6] Stricter kosher standards were promoted and enforced. Television and movies, acceptable leisure pursuits among American Orthodox Jews at the time, were regarded by these new Hasidim as dangerous distractions from the Torah life and were immediately banned. The adoption of Hasidic styles of dress, rooted to some degree in Jewish law but mostly in Eastern European custom, also served to distinguish the Hasidim from the goyim—a category that, for them, included not only non-Jews but Reform and secular Jews as well.[7] And, with the authority to administer their own educational institutions, these communities opened schools, or yeshivas. Aside from fulfilling state-mandated requirements in basic English and math, these yeshivas focused almost exclusively on religious education, rendered in Yiddish (and, for the boys, Biblical Hebrew). Any subject matter that could be seen as contradicting or undermining the Hasidic worldview was excluded from the curriculum.

The efforts of these new immigrants were so successful that, in less than twenty years, Williamsburg—and, to a lesser degree, Crown Heights—had become a thriving Hasidic community, with houses of worship and study for men, and ritual baths for women. Then, in the 1960s, in reaction to the growing numbers of blacks and Latinos moving into these areas, those residents who could afford it began moving to more established, socially desirable Jewish neighborhoods, such as Flatbush and Boro Park,[8] bringing their attitudes, lifestyles, and institutions with them.[9] The Bobover rebbe himself moved to Boro Park from Crown Heights in 1966.

While some in Boro Park resented the influx and ultimately moved out, Yossi's grandfather admired these new Hasidim and grew interested in becoming more like them. Slowly, he began changing his appearance, eschewing goyish or "modern" styles of dress in favor of the Hasidim's dark suits and white shirts. He even grew a beard and started donning a *bekishe*, the long silk caftan worn by men on Shabbos, in shul. When the Bobover school opened in the neighborhood, he sent his then twelve-year-old son—Yossi's father—there to learn. And though Yossi's grandmother had no special feeling for these newcomers, whom she considered "extreme Europeans," she went along with her husband and the neighborhood, covering her hair and beginning to dress more modestly.

By the time Yossi's father was ready for marriage, Boro Park had gone, as Egon Mayer has noted, from an American-Jewish community in which Jews could become Americanized and still remain Jewish, to a much more self-consciously Jewish community.[10] This transformation was no doubt aided by the growing emphasis on ethnic identity and pride that was influencing the larger culture at the time. And so, as Boro Park was becoming more Jewish and less American, Yossi's father was becoming a full-fledged Hasid. And, like most of those in the changed neighborhood, whether native-born or refugees, he intended to raise his children in this new "tradition." They would dress in the Hasidic manner, attend Hasidic schools, speak Yiddish, and, unlike him, they would not be exposed to television or movies or other types of people, even other types of Jews. And they would certainly not celebrate Thanksgiving. They would have no choice.

And so it had been for Yossi.

To be sure, there were things that Yossi liked about the way he grew up: the warmth and excitement of certain holidays and celebrations, which "gave life zest," "lit a fire under your ass," and made some men literally shake with love for God; the Eastern European food—especially *cholent* and herring—that topped the Sabbath table every week; his time spent schmoozing with his friends at the *beis medrash*, or religious study hall, over endless cups of coffee and cigarettes. But, as Yossi saw it, to enjoy these pleasures, he didn't have to be religious, or even believe in God, and he certainly didn't have to live the kind of life his father, and the people in his community, believed he should.

Indeed, after the demise of Yossi's short-lived arranged marriage, it had become increasingly difficult for him to imagine a life within the community at all. He saw that most Hasidim were, as he described it, "on the express train," getting married young and immediately starting a family that could grow to have as many as fifteen children in almost as many years. Divorce, still a source of stigma, though slightly less so in recent years, thrust one out onto the subway platform, with no clear sense of which train to hop next. Now Yossi was on the platform and, without the heavy baggage of a wife and children, he realized it was a place he was grateful to be.

It would be easy to blame the failure of Yossi's marriage on the fact that he and his wife were young when they got engaged (barely twenty), that they had met only twice before they wed, and that neither had ever been alone with a member of the opposite sex who was not a relative, much less been on any kind of date. But the truth is that almost every Hasidic young person marries this way, and most of those marriages remain intact. What ultimately ended Yossi's marriage was that he bought a TV.

It wasn't just the TV itself that was a problem, although it certainly *was* a problem, given its potential to contaminate the household with images of the corrupt, secular society, even though Yossi planned to use it only to watch rental videos. More important, though, was what the act of bringing it into the house revealed to his unsuspecting wife about the kind of person Yossi was and, more ominously, the kind of person he might become. After all, if he was "open-minded" enough to watch rented movies, then there was no way of knowing what other things he might do. It was a slippery slope, and, without firm knowledge of his own limits, Yossi might not know where to stop: watching videos at home might lead to other transgressions (books, magazines, nonkosher food, God knows what) and away from the 613 commandments that he was bound to observe as a religious Jew.

If only the matchmaker had dug a little deeper, he might have discovered a few red flags, like the fact that in high school, Yossi was bored by the exclusive curriculum of religious study. Curious about the world he saw every day on the streets of New York City, but in which he was forbidden to participate, Yossi had secretly taken himself to various libraries, reading everything he could get his hands on about American and Eastern European Jewish history, as well as the works of Isaac Bashevis Singer, Mendele Mokher Sefarim, Sholem Asch, and other Yiddish writers. Maybe the matchmaker would have learned that Yossi's grandmother had let him watch *Three Stooges* videos as a child, and that she had also shown him photographs of herself as a young married woman (before she had fifty grandchildren), dressed in a short skirt, her hair uncovered, holding hands with her husband. Maybe he would have understood that Yossi, though certainly attached to the Hasidic culture in which he had grown up, did not see why, in the land of freedom and opportunity, he should be consigned to a ghetto—particularly when he wanted more than anything to be able to live like "a regular American."

The most obvious sign of trouble should have been the fact that Yossi had been introduced to seven girls (all unmarried women in the community are referred to as "girls")—an unusually high number—before he agreed to marry his wife. Indeed, this would have been a decisive strike against him in the eyes of prospective in-laws, if he hadn't been the eldest son of a learned man, and a scholar in his own right: among the Hasidim, religious scholarship confers more prestige on men than even wealth.

The problem was, these introductions always turned Yossi into a nervous wreck. Sitting across the dining room table from a total stranger, with a few soda bottles and plastic cups between them, Yossi never knew what to say. Because there is such extreme sex segregation in the Hasidic world, and also because boys and girls don't learn the same things in school, their daily lives unfold in what often feels like two different worlds.

But neither could Yossi speak about anything he had learned outside of his religious studies, during these meetings, because revealing that he did *that* kind of reading might instantly alienate a nice religious girl and taint him in the eyes of other potential mates, as well; people always talked. He often wished that there were some kind of sign, a hand signal or a wink of an eye, that he could use to let the girl know that he was more open. As it was, though, talking honestly about these things was just too risky. It was much safer to stick to discussing which yeshiva his children would to go to, and what kind of hair covering his wife would wear, once they were married.

Yossi suspected that this entire process was not exactly conducive to the development of romance, let alone love. But the people in his community did not believe in love, or not in romantic love, at least. First and foremost, marriage was a partnership, a division of labor organized to ensure the perpetuation of the Jewish family and community. Over time, and in the common pursuit of this goal, the bond between man and wife would grow, even if openly expressing affection in public would always be considered too immodest, and thus inappropriate. Despite his apprehension, Yossi had no idea how he might avoid this fate. And at least the promise of regular—if highly regulated—sex, something he had been fantasizing about for years, gave him something to look forward to.

Young Hasidim are formally taught almost nothing about sex until the weeks immediately before their wedding, when young men and women attend classes taught by specially designated members of the community. Those who have had the advantage of an especially savvy older or married sibling, had access to pornography, or, tragically, been the victims of sexual abuse may have some prior knowledge of the subject. But many are shaken by what they learn, and some—especially the most sheltered boys—actually faint on the spot after hearing what they will have to do on their wedding nights. Yossi was certainly wiser to things than the fainters, but that did not make his wedding night any easier. After a day of fasting, followed by the ceremony, a huge meal, lots of alcohol, and dancing until four in the morning, he and his wife were expected to consummate the marriage. They were armed with little more than a printed instruction sheet, which detailed mainly those acts they were *not* allowed to perform. Yossi's wife was understandably nervous, as was he. But she knew she had to oblige and so, instruction sheet in hand, Yossi did his best also, although in truth he felt more like "a contractor trying to install an air conditioner" than a groom becoming one with his beloved bride.

Things only went downhill from there, with disagreements over whether Yossi would study or work (his wife wanted him to work) and then, once that was resolved (he went to work), long awkward silences born out of a complete lack of common conversational ground. Yossi began trying to stay out as late as possible, spending time after work in the religious study hall, hanging out with his friends, while his unhappy wife passed the time on the phone with a friend or a sister. Often he wouldn't come home until she was ready for bed.

And then came the TV.

Yossi actually bought the combination TV-VCR because he thought it might ease things between his wife and him. Maybe if they sat down and watched movies together, they would find something to talk about, to enjoy as a couple. At least he wouldn't feel so lonely in his own home. But, as it turned out, his wife didn't see things this way. She believed, as she had been taught, that television had no place in a Hasidic home. And so, after a series of unproductive sessions with a marriage counselor (whose main suggestions were that the couple play Monopoly together and that Yossi bring his wife flowers on the Sabbath), she picked up and left him. Although he knew he was supposed to feel bad about this, Yossi was actually, in his own words, "high as a kite." His wife had pulled the emergency brake, and the express had ground to a halt in the station. Now, with the divorce finalized and his stock in the community permanently lowered, it might just be the right time to find a train headed in another direction.

After finishing the potato chips and Hawaiian Punch, Yossi quit his park bench; it was time to get himself uptown to the party. But before heading to the subway, he put his kippah into the plastic bag he was carrying and chucked the bag into a nearby garbage can. Doing this, Yossi didn't feel that he was rejecting Judaism, or even Hasidism per se, although he knew full well that it certainly would have looked that way to anyone from his community.

Of course, it would have been useless for Yossi to try to explain to people like his father why he no longer wanted to wear the garb, especially because, among the Hasidim, there seemed to be no distinction between the religion and the culture. Wearing certain clothes, for example, was regarded more as a religious commandment handed down from God—like Sabbath observance and the kosher laws—than a socially constructed and historically bound custom. Indeed, many people in the community probably would have had fewer problems with Yossi's lack of belief than with his decision to remove his beard and stop wearing the clothes; after all, Orthodox Judaism has always placed more emphasis on ritual performance than on belief ("orthoprax," he had once heard it called). In fact, there was the pervasive notion in the community that someone who was going off the path might be brought back merely by acting "as if." At least the clothes and the dietary laws kept one from being able to fit in and mingle too much with the *goyim*—hanging out, for example, in Washington Square Park, listening to music and looking at pretty, immodestly dressed girls.

But, in the end, Yossi's objection to the garb was not primarily ideological. It was true that he didn't believe, and that wearing the clothes or adhering to the practices had no religious meaning for him anymore. More than that, however, Yossi was tired of his own false advertising. Sure, bus drivers called him "rabbi" as they excused his prop of an empty Metro Card and let him ride for free, a nice perk of the outfit; if he had learned anything in his community, it was how to "do *shtick*" with money. But then there were those like the apparently nonreligious woman who saw him buying a magazine in Barnes and Noble one Saturday and launched into a very loud speech about how inappropriate it was for him to be using money on Shabbos, which is against Jewish law. And there was also the fact that most of the pretty girls he tried to talk to seemed to relate to him as if he were either an alien from another galaxy or some rare exotic species *(Homo hasidus)*, too holy for mundane thoughts or conversation.

Never mind that, underneath the garb, Yossi was just a guy who liked Adam Sandler movies and country music, who wanted to know firsthand what kind of food people from other cultures ate at their parties, and what kind of jokes they told. And who wanted more than anything to go on dates with girls who would find him funny and attractive and might even want to have sex with him—though he had no idea what he would actually say to them to get them there.

The main thing was that, despite what all of his teachers and his parents had tried to drill into him, Yossi didn't believe that, as a Jew, he was really much different from anyone else, and he certainly didn't believe that he was any better. In fact, he had long had an intuitive sense that people were all just people, that "you could have *peyos* down to your *tuchus*, but in the end you're still really just like anyone else, black, white, or Chinese." These feelings were only confirmed for him by the many hours he had spent secretly watching *Oprah* on his grandmother's old black-and-white TV.

Of course, none of this meant that Yossi didn't identify as a Jew—with his background, what else could he possibly be? In fact, his extensive reading of Jewish history had shown him that, throughout time, Jews had found many different ways of being religious, and yet other ways of being secular while retaining a Jewish identity. Yossi didn't hate his community (although the way he was treated during his marriage and divorce had certainly made him bitter) or the Jewish religion. He simply longed for a life with fewer restrictions and more openness and tolerance. He even imagined that in his new life, come Friday night, he would "pop into" various shuls, just to see the different ways other Jews worshipped, although afterwards he might decide to go out for an emphatically nonkosher cheeseburger.

When Yossi arrived at the party, the Yiddishists were almost as stunned as the barber. Maybe even more so. Immediately someone suggested they drink a *l'chaim*, and another person asked whether there was a special prayer for such an occasion. Within Yossi's community, sitting *shiva*—the ritual of mourning when a relative dies—would have been the only plausible choice, and often was, in these situations. But everyone said he looked great. Yossi was thrilled, and the party went on late into the night, with lively talk about politics and film. Still, by the time it was all over, no one had made any mention of a job, and offers of a spare couch or a corner of rug were nowhere forthcoming.

It occurred to Yossi that perhaps he had misjudged these people. With his newly "modern" look, maybe he was no longer so appealing to the Yiddishists, who seemed to have regarded him, before, like one of the stuffed animals in the cases at the Museum of Natural History. In fact, while they had never hesitated to ask him to give them tours of his neighborhood, the Yiddishists always managed to make Yossi feel somehow inferior to them. They seemed to delight in their own stilted and formal version of Yiddish, even making fun of the living, breathing language that had shaped—and was in turn constantly being reshaped by—people like Yossi on the streets of Hasidic neighborhoods every day. In his mounting desperation, Yossi began to consider whether he would be better off being a Hasidic "somebody"—a quirky misfit whom everybody in the community might pity or scorn but at least know by name, and whom outsiders would find intriguing, if not exactly fully human—than the secular nobody he now worried that he was about to become.

Yossi realized that he had no place to go. And without his beard, his peyos, without even his kippah, it would be very hard to go back to Brooklyn, to go back home.

Yossi walked to the subway station and waited for a train heading downtown. His stomach began to churn. He still liked the way he looked whenever he caught sight of his reflection in the subway car windows, but he knew that his sister's reaction would not be quite so positive. He needed time to think about how he would handle the situation, what he would say to her, how he would act. He decided to give himself some time to think at a bar on the fringes of his neighborhood he had recently begun frequenting—a place run by Italian Americans and a refuge for other "open-minded" (and sometimes truly troubled) Hasidim, including a divorced woman named Breindel, who liked to remove her wig and relax with a drink and a cigarette. With what Yossi saw as great chutzpah, Breindel never missed an opportunity to scold him for being in the bar, proclaiming that it wasn't "modest" for a man dressed in Hasidic garb to be seen in such a place.

At the bar, all the staff knew Yossi as "Joey" ("Yossi" was apparently too foreign to get their tongues around). Now, when he walked in, nobody even recognized him. But then he opened his mouth, and as soon as she heard his familiar Yiddish accent and his nervous, though infectious, laugh, the bartender threw her arms across the bar and gave Yossi a big hug. She told him he looked "awesome" and on the spot invented a drink in celebration of his transformation. It contained four different kinds of alcohol, including something blue that Yossi couldn't identify. In honor of him, it was christened "The Joey."

Two Joeys later, Yossi knew he had no choice but to go home. As he walked through the dark streets of his neighborhood, he passed a few people he knew. Hasidim are notorious night owls, with their weddings and other celebrations often going on into the wee hours, so there were people on the street. As in the bar, however, none of them recognized him, thank God.

When Yossi finally reached home, he rang the buzzer and turned around, with his back to the door. His sister came to let him in and immediately asked what was wrong. Without turning toward her, Yossi assured his sister that everything was fine, that he had shaved his beard and cut off his peyos, but that she shouldn't worry, there was no problem. She begged him to turn around and, after he did, she burst into tears. She asked him where his kippah was, and he told her that he didn't have it. Because she had a friend staying over, she tried her best to contain herself, to stay calm. She asked him to hold the door and then disappeared into the house, returning with a pair of pantyhose for him to put on his head, so that it should not be uncovered, which is against Hasidic custom.

Trying not to increase her hysteria, Yossi complied and put the pantyhose on his head. He felt ridiculous.

"I'm scared," his sister said, trying to compose herself. "You look scary."

"I don't look scary because I shaved," Yossi told her, hoping some humor would lighten the situation. "I look scary because I have a pair of *pantyhose* on my head."

It didn't work. His sister was a mess. So Yossi ducked inside and went quickly to his cramped, tiny room. Sitting on his narrow single bed, he was left to contemplate what he had done, and what he would do next. Maybe this would all have worked out better, he told himself, if only he had known someone else in the same position; maybe the two of them could have hatched a plan together. As it was, Yossi felt very alone.

Little did Yossi know that night that he wasn't nearly as alone as he felt. If only I had known him then, and known what I do now, I would have been able to tell him that there were actually many people out there struggling with the same problems, some as close as a few blocks away. And not a few of them were in far worse situations than he, with spouses, children, and financial responsibilities—and sometimes even with lingering fears of God's wrath.

I could have told him about people like Steinmetz, the twenty-four-year-old bibliophile, who spends his days working in a small Judaica store in his community and—unbeknownst to his "narrow-minded" wife, or the members of his highly respected rabbinical family—his days off anxiously evading discovery in the library of the Conservative Jewish Theological Seminary. A religious man who first became curious when he went to Israel at sixteen to attend yeshiva, Steinmetz has never been to a movie theater, visited a bar, or even watched TV, for fear of where any of that could lead him. Indeed, his biggest pleasure in life is to sit at the library—which is where I first met him—and pore over heretical books about Spinoza and the *Haskalah* (Jewish Enlightenment), while dreaming of an escape from his community into the world of modern Orthodox Zionists. However, with his impressive *yiches*, or family pedigree, and his kids, who will need good *shidduchim*, or matches, Steinmetz is certain that this escape will remain a dream. And so, for the foreseeable future, he has resigned himself to staying in the "tight cage" of his lonely life.

Then there is P., the self-identified *apikoros*, or heretic, who first found knowledge on the Internet—he was a believer until he logged on and clicked around—and now uses his blog to proclaim his lack of belief in God, and to chronicle how he watches movies, reads books, desecrates the Sabbath, visits massage parlors and strip clubs, and eats *treiyf*, or nonkosher food, behind his wife's back. So great is P.'s fear of exposure that he agreed to meet me only after I had e-mailed him on the Sabbath (which is forbidden, as it involves using electricity), thereby unintentionally proving that I was not a spy from his community.

Although he is desperate to change his life, P. is burdened by the knowledge that doing so would ruin the lives of his children: kids whose parents "go off" become *nebs* (*nebbishes*, or nothings) and rejects, the lowest of the low. Yet he is also plagued by the fear that, in the end, he might be doing them even more harm by raising them to live a life he doesn't believe in. His goal is to get very rich—which he is trying hard to do in the construction business—so that he might be able to ensure good matches for his children, even if he is discovered. These days, money can often redeem even the worst sins of the father.

Tormented by guilt over lying to his wife, P. is quick to note the "pathetic" irony that, while his great-grandparents risked their lives to practice their religion in secret, he must sneak around and hide just to be free *not* to practice his.

Or I could tell Yossi about Dini. . . .

Chapter Two

Wigged Out

When Dini enters the bar, she is dressed modestly: long dark skirt, long-sleeved sweater, ash-blonde wig covering her hair. She bids me hello but doesn't stop to sit down, heading straight to the bathroom instead. When she emerges several minutes later—in tight jeans and a tank top, her real hair jet black, curly, and flying—all eyes are trained in her direction. No one would ever guess she was a Hasidic Jew. Well, sort of.

Even though she grew up in Williamsburg, and is married to a Hasidic man, today Dini feels pretty far from her Hasidic life. To some extent, this is because she is in fact far from it—geographically, at least—living with her husband and young son in a Jewish neighborhood in Queens. But the distance she has traveled is also marked by the difference in the way she thinks and feels, both about life these days and about the life she was raised to lead—and is still trying to shed.

For as long as she can remember, Dini, the oldest child in a family of ten, wanted information. She wanted to know about what went on in others people's lives and heads, both in her community and outside of it. She wanted to know what people really thought about things, and how they felt, especially women. For example, when Dini was a little girl, she always wanted to know whether married women in her community missed feeling the breeze in their hair, being stuck wearing scarves and wigs over their shaved heads all the time. She also wondered whether they minded always riding in the back seat of the car, instead of up front, next to their male drivers. Having to forgo the passenger seat after girlhood to avoid sitting next to a man seemed to her like an unfair demotion. She was also very curious about how her own body worked; seeing so many pregnant women all the time prompted a lot of questions. As a teenager, Dini became even more curious—about things like love and passion and sex. And, of course, she wanted to know all about the outside world: what seeing a movie was like, how it felt to wear pants, what went on inside non-Jewish homes, and if they were really so unclean, as she had been told. Of course, none of this information was easy to come by for a young Hasidic girl. She was not supposed to have such questions—or to read nonreligious books, see movies, watch television, or listen to the radio; she was forbidden any contact with the opposite sex, save for brothers and uncles and cousins; and she was taught to respect and observe the laws of modesty.

Tznius, or modesty, is considered one of the most fundamental and important values of Hasidic womanhood, creating expectations not only for a woman's outward appearance, but also for her thoughts and behavior, including her speech. The concept derives from a verse in Psalm 45 that states that "the entire glory of the King's daughter is on the inside." Within strict Orthodoxy, this has been interpreted to mean that the true nature of the Jewish woman is private, making her the keeper of the Jewish home and family, the one who guards its purity and ensures its strength and perpetuation. In schools and lectures,[1] teachers often support this association between femaleness and the private realm with the idea that men create by giving up a part of themselves, while women do so by taking something in. This fact of reproductive anatomy is then used to explain why it is that men must go out to pray together, while women, left to develop their inner qualities—the nurturing tendencies and intuition, which apparently exist naturally within them—can pray alone, at home, while minding the house and children.

To properly fulfill her role, according to the laws of tznius, a woman must always be careful to be modest in her self-presentation and her actions. This does not mean, however, that she should refrain from expressing her thoughts or opinions, or from asserting herself within the domestic sphere. Rather, the laws of tznius teach that a woman should not seek publicity for her accomplishments or good deeds. She should not speak on immodest topics, or disparagingly about others. And she should not draw attention to herself by laughing too loudly, appearing to enjoy herself too much, or flaunting her God-given beauty, which she should preserve for her husband's eyes alone to see, within the sanctity of their marriage. Indeed, Hasidic ideology places a heavy burden on women to thwart male sexual temptation.

So strong is this ideal, so central in Hasidic thought to the maintenance and continuation of the community, that young girls are often instructed that "Tznius and women are inseparable," and then told gory stories about Jewish women in history who opted to starve to death, or be tortured, before they would lose their purity. One particular favorite describes a group of women who fastened their skirts to their legs with pins in order to preserve their modesty as they were dragged through the streets to their deaths.

In practice, among the Hasidim this emphasis on tznius translates into strict regulations regarding styles of dress, and within Dini's community, this meant wearing dark blue or thick, flesh-toned stockings with seams up the back (to demonstrate that one was indeed wearing stockings), skirts far below the knee, and shirts covering the collarbone and elbow. Pants were never an option, as the Torah commands that women not wear men's clothing, and vice versa. For Dini, obeying the laws of tznius also meant that immediately after her wedding, a woman's head was shorn of its sexually tempting hair, and that thereafter she wore a head covering—a scarf; a wig, or *shaitel;* or a *shpitzel,* a partial wig consisting only of a front piece, typically covered by a small pillbox hat. To ensure that not a strand of her own hair was visible in public, she would likely also tweeze any stray hairs on her face, near her hairline.

Within Hasidic communities, the laws of tznius are used to explain why men and women cannot mix together in public, or sit side-by-side at lectures or presentations, on buses, in cars, or even at weddings. In fact, in instances where mixed attendance is required, men and women are separated by a wall or curtain, or *mechitza*. Tznius is also the reason that a bride and groom don't ever touch one another, or spend time alone together, until after they are married. A concern with tznius prohibits fathers from attending their daughters' school plays, as the sound of women singing can lead to uncontrollable male sexual arousal. It is also why men and women working together in offices are advised to refer to each other in the third person, and to keep the door open whenever they are alone together. Tznius is the explanation given in Dini's former community for prohibiting women from driving—the temptation of all that freedom could lead them somewhere immodest. It explained why, if a woman was not properly covered during prayer, she would have to consider her prayers wasted—breaking God's laws of modesty would surely cause her prayers to fall on His deaf ears. And tznius is also why, when Dini was growing up, nobody ever learned the words for genitals, or openly discussed those parts of the body at all. And they certainly never discussed how those body parts might be linked to feelings and emotions, until it was absolutely necessary—that is, a few weeks before the wedding.

Dini remembers her prewedding sex lesson very well, particularly for how technical it was. Her instructor didn't talk at all about love—that would come later, she assured Dini—or desire, but only about the laws surrounding sexual relations and about what went where. But because Dini had been so curious for so long, she was actually a little excited on her wedding night, even though she wasn't exactly sure whether or not she was attracted to her husband, or that she even knew what attraction was supposed to feel like. Despite her excitement, however, the experience turned out to be frightening and filled with embarrassment, as well as generous amounts of lubricant, which, like most Hasidic grooms, her husband had been instructed to purchase at the local drugstore by his "sex rabbi." He was also instructed by that same rabbi to touch and hold his wife only during sex, so as not to risk spilling his seed when there would be no chance of conception.

Dini's marriage went along well enough at first, even though her husband was a "total stranger." He was also a nice guy. While they were engaged, the two had barely any contact with each other, save for the two celebrations that are customarily held to mark the engagement. Even at these events, he never spoke directly to her, and whenever she came to his house to visit with his female relatives before the wedding, he would leave the apartment—all behavior typical of a Hasidic boy before marriage. All of Dini's friends and female relatives focused, and wanted her to focus, on the flowers and engagement presents she was receiving, on the ring she had been given, on the furniture and dishes and silverware that would arrive as gifts after the wedding. But Dini couldn't understand why everybody made all of that seem so much more important than having a little contact with the man with whom she had agreed to share her life.

Of course, none of Dini's fiancé's behavior had anything to do with him, with what kind of person he was or how he felt about Dini. It was all about custom, the way things were done. In fact, marriage actually represented a kind of freedom to Dini. It meant that she no longer had to take care of her younger siblings at home, nor obey her parents' strict rules. Indeed, while her father, who worked in the diamond district on Forty-seventh Street, often read the newspaper and sometimes even magazines (which Dini discovered and sneaked when her parents weren't home, staring at the pictures of women, whose faces were always blotted out of all the Hasidic papers), he did not afford his children the same opportunity. This is not at all atypical in Hasidic homes. The thinking goes something like this: A young child, who does not yet have the proper foundation in the Hasidic value system and way of life, can very easily be led astray by any contact at all with the outside world. An adult, however—in these communities, anyone who is married—presumably has internalized the Hasidic worldview completely and unproblematically enough to be able to withstand at least limited contact with secular culture: a newspaper, maybe certain books, possibly even a movie.

This way of thinking tends to lead to situations in which parents often engage in activities in secret together, away from home or behind closed doors, in order to avoid the risk of exposing their children to anything that might "confuse" them (a word commonly used among Hasidim in this context) or cause them to question or rebel. Of course, such parents have an additional motivation for keeping these kinds of "nonkosher" activities under wraps: the Hasidic system of marriage. If parents allow themselves to get a reputation for being "corrupt," their children's marriage prospects may suffer, so making sure to conceal any behavior that could undermine their chances becomes extremely important.

Dini's parents didn't exactly hide her father's newspaper reading from her, although she certainly hid some things from them, like the fact that she sometimes took the subway into the city to check out the short skirts and tank tops at H&M, fantasizing about what she would do in them if she could actually wear them. Her secrets included hanging out in record stores, just to be able to hear popular music, even though it was composed by non-Jews, whose impure souls, she was taught, would infect the purity of her own through their melodies. And, of course, she *never* let on to anyone at all that she also sometimes masturbated. For Hasidic boys, masturbation is considered a serious sin because it involves the "destruction of seed," but there is no explicit prohibition in the Torah against female masturbation. However, this is not to say that masturbation is something that is remotely encouraged or even discussed formally among Hasidic women. Aside from anything else, attitudes about the body and sexuality fostered by the laws of tznius make it a difficult thing for many even to contemplate. But Dini always felt she was different, although she didn't know this for sure, because everyone was so good at hiding things; she could never really know anything about anyone else. Like her husband.

Much to Dini's happy surprise, it turned out that her husband was pretty open-minded. He was a believer, certainly, as was she, but he had also done some things he wasn't supposed to. In fact, over time, the two of them began to tell each other about all the rebellious things they had ever done. Dini, certain that she was impressing her husband with her small but not insignificant record of transgressions, was surprised and intrigued when, after letting her go on and on about her few trips to the record store, her husband reached into his wallet and pulled out ticket stubs for fifteen movies he had seen surreptitiously. Soon after that, her husband brought home a TV and a VCR (covered in garbage bags, so the neighbors wouldn't suspect). They began listening to his favorite music in the car. And, soon after that, they bought a computer.

Among the Hasidim, using the Internet had become the latest sin in a seemingly ever-growing list. Every week there were new flyers posted around Williamsburg, warning of its dangers:

> *The terrible sickness* [a ubiquitous euphemism for cancer] *that is going around today and creating many orphans has never been such an issue as it is today. People are asking, why is it so? The reason is because of the Internet and magazines. Unfortunately, many Jewish homes have the Internet and it is like a burning fire that needs to be extinguished. If you know anyone who has the Internet convince him to drop it. And if you need it for business purposes you should just get J Net* [a filtering service].

Apparently unconvinced of its cancer-causing properties, but certain that people would heed the implicit call to rat out their neighbors, Dini and her husband also signed up for an Internet connection. Every time they would use their TV to watch movies, Dini would first cover her windows with dark towels and then go outside, just to make sure that nobody passing by their apartment building could see the cool blue light of the cathode ray. Dini's husband also began renting movies in Manhattan and bringing them home in a bag from a Duane Reade drugstore, which he kept just for that purpose.

Dini loved watching movies, particularly the ones that told the stories of people from other cultures with whom she could identify, like the couple having an arranged marriage in *Monsoon Wedding*, or the girl in *Bend It Like Beckham*, who was fighting against tradition so she could play soccer competitively. And Dini also became totally hooked on old episodes of *Sex and the City* she got her husband to rent on DVD so she could watch them on the computer. The clothes were amazing, and everyone looked so beautiful to her, just as they did when, as a little girl, she would stare—against her parents' admonitions—out of the car window whenever they drove through a non-Jewish neighborhood, wishing one of those smiling, non-Jewish families on the street would adopt her. She would imagine how they would come and take her right out of her crowded apartment, where people yelled a lot and never really listened, and into their blonde, American lives.

Did non-Jewish women, women outside her community, really have lives like those in *Sex and the City*, full of excitement and glamour and so many men? Dini couldn't be sure. But sometimes it all looked a little scary, with no rules for guidance. All of the videos were giving Dini a crash course, but all of the worrying whether the neighbors would hear them, or the whirring sound of the tapes rewinding, was starting to make her angry. And she was also starting to feel angry about the uncomfortable thick stockings, and her itchy shaved head, and the long skirts that looked so unflattering—even though she wasn't supposed to be concerned with all of that.

Sometimes, when her husband was watching a movie she wasn't interested in, Dini would log on to the Internet and explore the world. At first, she went to sites with information about different religions and cultures: Buddhism, Hinduism, even something called the Tao. In between, she clicked on links and ads and registered for a free e-mail account; within a few days, her mailbox was filled with information about how to get cheap Viagra and enlarge her penis. Then, emboldened by her solo virtual travels, Dini began to lurk in chat rooms, looking for others in her situation, and, when she had lurked enough, she joined the chat herself. Soon, screen names like BobovBabe and orthorebel were popping up in her IM window, asking for her a/s/l (age, sex, and location) and offering her theirs. A lot of these people seemed to be religious guys who wanted only to talk about or arrange a meeting for sex, which to Dini was both shocking and intriguing. But a few of these IMers seemed to understand where she was coming from, and Dini found she could really open up. And then FreidOut turned her on to the then small group of Hasidic bloggers, all of them men, who were posting scathing critiques about their communities and documenting their double lives online.

Reading these posts almost felt like looking at pornography. Dini couldn't get enough, identifying with so much of what these bloggers were writing—although, unlike a lot of them, she definitely did believe in God. Dini wanted desperately to meet some of these bloggers in person, or at least maybe talk to them on the phone. But she didn't dare try. Never in her life had she had a male friend and besides, she knew that her husband would freak out. And if anyone from the community found out she was doing this, it would be the end. Still, hearing the stories of others was making her ever more aware of how stifled she felt, and soon enough these virtual travels weren't enough for Dini. She wanted to go experience the outside world for herself, in the flesh.

Throughout this time, of course, Dini was having sex with her husband the Hasidic way: observing the laws of family purity, or *Taharas Hamishpacha,* and refraining from any physical contact with him during her period and in the week that followed. During this time, a woman is considered to be in *niddah,* or ritually impure, due to uterine bleeding, and complete physical separation from her husband is required. In Hasidic families, when a woman is in niddah, it means that she cannot hug, hold hands with, or touch her husband at all, and that she is prohibited from even passing things to him. At this time, husbands and wives do not spend any time in the same bed, lest even accidental, potentially arousing touching occur.

Even now, Dini recalls how incredibly important it was to everyone to make sure that her wedding was not scheduled when she would be in niddah, preventing the consummation of the marriage that night, and forcing her to endure the embarrassment of having everyone present know that she was "unclean" because her husband would obviously avoid touching her during their wedding dance. Looking back, Dini laughs at all the worrying she did over this. Indeed, she now wonders how she could have cared about not being able to touch her husband that night. As it turned out, when they actually got the chance to dance together, it felt like nothing more to Dini than touching a wall, although she tried to force herself to feel something more, given what a big moment that dance was supposed to be in her life. Dini still doesn't feel much of anything during sex with her husband, although she likes it when he hugs her.

The time of ritual impurity is over on the woman's seventh "clean" day, or the seventh day after the cessation of the menstrual period. In order to know for sure that all bleeding has ended, Hasidic women are taught to wear white underwear, which shows stains better, and also to use a special cloth, which is inserted like a tampon, and which, when removed, will show any evidence of residual bleeding. If the cloth comes out clean, physical contact between a husband and wife may resume. At those times when women themselves are not exactly sure about whether their periods have ended, it is customary to take the matter to a rabbi with special training in determining the precise nature of any spotting or stains. To do this, a husband will bring his wife's underwear, or the white cloth, to be looked at by such a specialist, who will hold it up to the light and, in a few seconds, make a ruling.

When it has been determined that a woman is clean, she must then go to the ritual bath, or the *mikvah*, to purify herself; indeed, Hasidic women are taught that this is one of the most important *mitzvot*, or commandments, that they follow,[2] particularly because they have complete control over its execution. Before a woman immerses herself in the water, her body must be scrubbed and then checked by the "mikvah lady," who scrutinizes her skin for any stray hairs, signs of unremoved nail polish, threads, dirt, or lint. If anything comes between a woman and the water, the ritual purification will be compromised.

From the very beginning, the whole idea of the mikvah made Dini a little uncomfortable. She knew all the arguments about how beautiful the ritual was, how exciting it could be to go to the mikvah in anticipation of the wonderful reunion she would have with her husband after her long, enforced separation, particularly if she were really in love. But Dini still didn't know what love was supposed to feel like, and she had no idea how to tell whether she was in love with her husband. Dini also felt very exposed having someone else inspect her body while she was naked, and watch over her as she dipped, making sure she did it properly. For someone who grew up in a community where a woman couldn't even show her knees or elbows, and a bathing suit was considered a "dirty" piece of clothing, this certainly seemed like a strange mitzvah to her. Indeed, having another person watch as her breasts bobbed up and down in the water could be quite humiliating.

Dini tells me that she has heard, in recent years, that mikvah ladies have been instrumental in the success of broader efforts to reach out to women who are the victims of domestic abuse. Indeed, because they see women without their clothes on, they are often the only people who ever become aware of telltale bruises or other marks on a woman's body. Dini now thinks that maybe this is the best thing to come out of the whole ritual.

About half a year into her marriage, Dini got a break from the mikvah, in the form of a pregnancy, and like many girls from her community, she was a mother by age twenty. For this, she found herself totally unprepared. After the birth of her son, Dini became extremely depressed. At the time, nobody bothered to tell her about postpartum depression, and she believed there was something terribly wrong with her. But, even beyond the depression, Dini knew deep down that she wasn't ready for a child. She still felt like a child herself, naïve about so many things, and wanting more and more to explore the outside world. She was miserable, and terrified that she would take her misery out on her child.

Over time, Dini realized that she needed help, and eventually she got it, in the form of therapy, which she sought outside of her community, on a recommendation from someone online. While she slowly started to feel a little more in control of herself, her life in the community was becoming more and more unbearable. In therapy, she was learning that she didn't have to live with all these restrictions, restrictions that she had always believed came from God, but was now beginning to think had merely been created by men. And, as much as she tried to feel love for her son, Dini was also resentful of having to suppress so much of herself to care for him. She was fed up with always having to watch herself, worrying about the length of her skirt, the stray, showing hairs, the thickness of her stockings, the glow from the TV, and the increasing stares and glares and whispers from the neighbors. Sometimes she and her husband would check themselves into a motel in New Jersey for a night, just to be able to watch a movie in peace.

Dini wanted desperately to move out of Williamsburg, but her husband had a good job in a small business there and couldn't afford to leave it. She would have to make do. And so, to ease the pressure, Dini started spending even more time online. She even tried to "meet" Muslim women and managed to find a few—none in places where women had to wear burkas, or were forbidden to attend school, but mostly teenage girls living in neighborhoods in Long Island or L.A. or Detroit, battling their immigrant parents over how they wanted to dress and what they wanted to do on the weekends. Dini could relate. Soon, "lol," "ttyl," "g2g," and "neway" became staples of her vocabulary, and, even though she never ended up actually meeting any of these women, somehow just knowing they were available inside that box made her feel better.

When the Internet wasn't enough, Dini began going out by herself, to a dark little bar outside the neighborhood, where she would order a drink, put money in the jukebox, and flirt with Tony, the muscular bartender. In time, Dini bought herself some short skirts and tank tops and shoes with high heels that she could wear outside the community. Her husband didn't like it, but in truth, his reaction wasn't very important to Dini. While she cared for him, and they got along well, she never felt that they had actually chosen each other. She and her husband hadn't married for love, she reasoned, so why should she be made to act that way?

Sometimes, they would leave the baby with relatives and go out to clubs and concerts, or even to the beach, although they were always paranoid the whole time, looking around for anyone who might recognize them, particularly considering Dini's outfits. Sometimes her husband wondered why she needed to wear such clothes. Did she want to pick up other guys? What was this all about?

Dini believes now that this wasn't really about picking up other men so much as it was about her need to feel sexy and attractive, like a "regular American girl," the type who would drive to the beach in a convertible, with music blaring and her hair blowing in the wind—just the opposite of how she felt in her long skirts and thick stockings and shaved head. In fact, in time, Dini decided that she wanted to stop shaving her head altogether and grow her hair long, keeping it tucked underneath her wig.

But before Dini had even begun to let her hair grow out, she had started getting a little more daring with her clothes in the neighborhood. She bought a few skirts that were a little shorter than "regulation," with a bit of a flounce, and also began wearing a thinner grade of stocking. Sometimes, even in Williamsburg, she dared to wear high-heeled shoes and boots. Waiting at the subway stop to go into the city, other women would look her over disdainfully, and sometimes even approach her, informing her that her skirt was too short or that her collarbone was exposed. Dini did everything she could to keep herself from punching them. After all, she kept all the commandments. What right was it of theirs to tell her how to look? What did they think they could do?

Well, somebody clearly did something, because not long after, Dini received a call from an anonymous man, telling her that she needed to "watch" the way she was dressing. Dini would have been furious about this call if she hadn't been in such shock, wondering what this was all about, and how this person had decided to pick on her. She had long heard rumors that there were some men in the community who were designated to enforce the rules, sometimes even beating up boys who got out of line, and she was terrified that this was one of them. But she also knew they couldn't actually do anything physical to her. She was a woman, after all. And she wasn't living in Afghanistan or Iran, a fate she had been hearing a lot about on the car radio lately. She had *some* rights.

Fortunately, Dini managed to avoid finding out what could have happened to her. Shortly after the phone call, her husband was offered a job with a company based in Queens, and they were finally able to move out of Williamsburg, to a more liberal community. Apparently, the job offer came just in time, because Dini discovered that the powers that be in the community were planning not to allow her to enroll her son in school there.

The move immediately gave Dini a tremendous feeling of liberation and relief. Many things that she could wear only outside of Williamsburg she can now wear every day, although she still has to be a little careful (hence, the quick change in the bar's bathroom when we met). She has also started to explore even more, reading books about Judaism, as well as biographies of women who've triumphed in the face of adversity, including Anne Frank. With this feeling of liberation, however, also came a tremendous amount of anger, which has quickly developed into a visceral hatred of "the whole thing"—her old community, its practices, its control over her body and her life. These days, she cannot even stand the sound of Yiddish, because of its associations with being controlled and prohibited from engaging with the outside world.

Recently, Dini has started venting to her husband more and more, and he has begun to think that his early tolerance served to foster the growth of a raging, unstoppable monster. He doesn't always understand why she is so angry, particularly since they are no longer living in their old community. And, while he remains open to some rebellious activity, he has become afraid she will go off the edge completely. He still has many friends and family back in Williamsburg, and he has no desire to lose them. He wishes she could just calm down.

But she can't. It enrages Dini that she gave up her virginity to a total stranger, even though she feels close to her husband now. At the time, of course, she didn't know anything about virginity, or about losing it. She just went along. Now she feels almost as if it was a form of socially sanctioned rape. And she has also begun to think about how all the men in the community got to sing and dance together, when she could only watch all the excitement from the women's section. These days, Dini is starting to feel that she was more of a second-class citizen in her old community than the "Daughter of Royalty" the teachers were so busy trying to convince her she was.

Of course, because she remains observant, Dini still goes to the mikvah, as she always has, but she sometimes breaches protocol, using her own sponge rather than the washcloth they provide. And she doesn't dunk as much as before. There is something that irks her about having to come home and present herself to her husband as "kosher for sex," as if she must submit to him, although she knows she doesn't have to, that he would never force her into it, and that Jewish law indeed prohibits that kind of duress. Maybe some of the stress around the whole issue comes from the fact that Dini wants to avoid having another child.

In fact, she has been on the pill for quite some time now, and because she is "done with rabbis" controlling her body, she didn't even go to one to get permission to use it. Her husband thinks that they should try one more time for a girl—some believe that the commandment to be fruitful and multiply requires at least one child of each sex, if not as many kids as possible—but Dini is resisting. She is worried, however, that God may just make it happen, perhaps to punish her or teach her something. As much as she is trying to get away from that way of thinking, she is finding it very hard. In her old community, people would say that if things went well, it was a reward for obeying God's laws. If something went wrong, it was probably just punishment for religious laxity.

Dini's idea of God is slowly evolving. She still believes in Him, but now He is a different kind of God from the one she grew up with. Her new God is a loving God, patient and understanding, a God with whom she can talk and who will listen. She doesn't pray to Him using Jewish prayers anymore, but rather thanks Him directly for what He has given her, or has helped her with. And she yells at Him when she is upset about something. Sometimes the old God, the one whose wrath she fears, pops up in her life, and the two do battle in her mind. Of course, Dini prefers the loving God, but also admits that His unconditional love makes it hard to know what He considers a sin. It is difficult to live without clear rules to guide one's behavior, and Dini believes this is why so many people who question or abandon Hasidic life can easily go from one extreme to the other. But the therapy is helping her with that.

Right now, Dini's big problem is that she doesn't know how to deal with her son. She doesn't want him to be confused, but she also dislikes a lot of what he is learning in school. He comes home and tells her that she shouldn't wear pants, that her blouse is open too low, or that she can or cannot do certain things on Shabbos. She would like to explain to him that she thinks all this is silly, but she has no idea how, or what it would do to his development. Even so, hearing all of this reminds her of the awful things her own teachers taught her in school.

One of the things Dini will never forget from her schooldays is that the teachers used a particular phrase to curse Hitler, and used that same phrase, and in the same breath, to curse Theodore Herzl, one of the early visionaries of Zionism. They made a direct parallel between the two men. Today, this embarrasses and angers Dini, and she is even growing to feel a little better about Israel's existence. At the same time, she also is bothered by the whole idea of "chosenness," that the Jews are a superior people. These days at least, Dini hates *all* the categories and divisions, the idea that the goyim are bad, that the artists in Williamsburg are dirty, or that it's unsafe to walk in Harlem.

Dini doesn't know what's going to happen with her life, where it's going to go, who she might become. She is certainly grateful for her husband's tolerance, and for the respect he has shown her throughout these past years, but she still feels "trapped and cheated" because of the things in life she has been denied. She believes that she should have been allowed to have a real boyfriend, to feel infatuation—even if, by definition, it's only temporary—but she doesn't want to have to give up her family in order to have these experiences. She would really like to get to know some other people in her position, for support and advice, not just on the Internet, but in person. She would like to see the way that they are handling things, how they are making their decisions and choices. But she is not sure she is ready yet. God might still get angry with her. Or someone from her old community might find out. She is not sure she is ready to take the plunge.

Chapter Three

Floating

The first few days after the shave were crazy, with Yossi's aunt begging and pleading with him to stay in the house until his beard grew back, so that nobody in the community "should know" what he had done. After all, if anyone saw him beardless, word would spread like wildfire, and then there would be no telling how it might affect the marriage chances of her unmarried children, let alone Yossi's younger brothers and sisters. If he just stayed inside, she told him, nobody would have to know anything. They could keep this whole *meshugas* to themselves. How long could it take for a beard to grow back, anyway? she yelled, less in rage than in desperation. Maybe a week or two, at the most? She had never actually known anyone who had shaved off his beard. She was ready to lock Yossi inside the house and stand guard at the front door.

For some reason, listening to his aunt's ranting and raving was much easier for Yossi than dealing with his sister, who couldn't stop crying. He tried to convince her that it was only hair, and that he was still the same person underneath the smooth face, but this didn't seem to work, and her crying continued unabated. His youngest cousin made a game of running up to Yossi and touching his chin, asking him over and over again why he had become a goy. Yossi thought his grandmother's reaction was the most reasonable of the bunch. She told him that she didn't see why he wanted to create so much trouble for himself, shrugged, and then said that without the beard he reminded her a little of her late brother. Nobody wanted to break the news to Yossi's father up in the mountains, however. They only needed to imagine his reaction to know that calling him right away would be a very bad idea. They all agreed that it would be best if they waited a while.

So, Yossi kept a low profile. During that first week, he tried not to go out too much, at least during the day. Instead, he waited around for some hair to show up on his face again. Because he had never shaved before, he, like his aunt, had no idea how long that might take. Mostly, Yossi spent his time in his room watching *Jerry Springer*, local news broadcasts, and reruns of *The Odd Couple* through a haze of bad reception on the tiny TV he had bought a few days after his family left for the mountains. When there was nothing interesting for him to watch on TV, he dipped into his growing porn collection (with his parents out of town, he had grown a little lax, accidentally leaving some of his magazines in plain sight for his horrified sister to see), or slept. Several times, he actually dreamed about being Oscar Madison. When he got hungry, Yossi made the only thing he knew how to cook: scrambled eggs and toast. He was convinced that his cholesterol would shoot through the roof. Now that he had finally gotten rid of his beard, he was probably going to drop dead from a heart attack.

And the *shreiing* continued. Yossi's aunt would show up at the apartment, sometimes as often as three times a day, occasionally even as late as two in the morning, after a wedding or a party, and yell: What on earth had possessed him to do this? Did he understand that he had now lost any hope of getting a halfway decent *shidduch,* that maybe, if he were very lucky, he would get someone stupid or a klutz with crossed eyes? Had he considered how this was going to affect anyone else before he acted so impulsively? Why did he have to go so extreme? And now what on earth was he going to do about a job?

Yossi tried not to react too much to this barrage. He knew his aunt was just very upset, that eventually she would calm down and stop yelling. He wasn't a fighter, like his father and younger brothers. During all those years in yeshiva, he had learned that the best way to get along was to stay quiet and keep his thoughts to himself. Boys who made trouble or asked too many questions were yelled at, and sometimes even hit, by the teachers. He had heard from some of the older guys in the community, particularly those who had studied in the Satmar community, about the especially harsh treatment meted out by teachers who had survived the Nazi camps. Given the likely strictness of their own European upbringings, and the horrors they had endured during the Holocaust, it was almost hard to blame them—although that certainly didn't make their harsh brand of discipline any easier to take. Thankfully, things were much better now, with some members of the community taking social work training, and all sorts of books coming out about how to raise children. This was an awareness that had clearly seeped into the community from the outside world. But Yossi's experience had made a big impression on him, and avoiding confrontation at all costs had become his preferred survival strategy.

So, while Yossi's aunt made herself hysterical, he just sat across from her, nodding his head and repeating the phrases "Right, right" and "No problem" over and over. He couldn't see the point in telling his aunt that he didn't give a damn about a shidduch, that he certainly had no intention of remarrying anytime soon—let alone with someone from the community—and that he was tired of having to live his whole life worrying about what other people were going to think of him. She wouldn't understand.

His aunt was right about the job issue, however. Yossi hadn't given it much thought before the shave, mainly because he had convinced himself that the Yiddishists were going to take care of that for him. But ever since that plan had "exploded like a huge stink bomb," he really didn't know what he was going to do for money. The problem was that finding work in the community would be much harder after news of his actions spread, which it inevitably would. There was little chance that anyone would hire him to tutor yeshiva boys again in the fall, his only source of income since his divorce. Who in the community would want to expose his children to someone who had fallen down so far?

But Yossi had almost no marketable skills he could use in the outside world, either. He had long thought that he would like to be a translator of Hebrew and Yiddish—that is, until a librarian friend at the pubic library had asked him to translate some of her grandfather's old letters from Yiddish into English. Of course, he understood everything perfectly, but when it came time to put the words down on paper in English, he had been so stumped by the spelling and grammar that he had been forced to make up an excuse about having bad handwriting, offer his apologies, and back out. It was a rude awakening.

During his marriage, Yossi had held a coveted job working as a cashier in an electronics store owned and staffed by Hasidim. The money and benefits were pretty good, but the work was mind numbing. Mostly, it consisted of ringing up people's purchases and verifying their credit card numbers. The majority of the men who worked there with Yossi cared mainly about making money, and few were intellectuals, closet readers, or film buffs, like Yossi. The closest they came was scanning Page Six and the Sports section of the *New York Post*, and secretly watching porn videos obtained from the Latino guy in shipping. Then, because the man who had hired Yossi was related to his wife, when the marriage was over, he lost the job, which was actually just fine with him. He didn't think he would have been able to stand a life of swiping credit cards and taking orders from a boss who couldn't even properly pronounce the word "credit."

With so few options, it was no mystery to Yossi why so many Hasidim he knew—even members of his own family—were on public assistance.[1] Unless a man was a big *macher* in retail or real estate, there was very little he could do to support so many children on so little formal education. Teaching in a yeshiva hardly paid enough, and those jobs were limited anyway. And even though having a large family was considered a religious obligation, Yossi didn't think that it was such an admirable thing, when one needed to take money from the government, or from others in the community, to support them. In fact, his own grandfather had been such a stickler about working for a living and paying his fair share, that he often told Yossi how flabbergasted he had been when someone from shul suggested he illegally obtain a second Social Security number for his recently married daughter. His grandfather seemed to want Yossi to know where he stood on the matter of work and handouts.

Over the years, Yossi had come to think of the men who had set up this system as "evil geniuses," bent on denying people a secular education so that they would be dependent on community support and government assistance—in other words, trapped. Of course, in reality, the story is a bit more complicated than that. Historically, the Hasidim had always valued work, a view that flows directly from the Hasidic understanding of God's relationship to the world. Hasidic theology holds that God is present not just in the spiritual realm, but in the material world as well. Consequently, Hasidim believe that an individual can achieve a spiritual connection to God through engagement in even the most mundane activities, including work. Indeed, it is their non-Hasidic, strictly Orthodox counterparts, known as the *Misnagdim* (or the "opponents" of Hasidism), who assign a primary value to Torah study, over and above everything else. The Misnagdim's emphasis on study reflects their belief that God has withdrawn His presence from the material world and is thus accessible to human beings exclusively through religious scholarship. While historically, the Misnagdim tended to disdain mundane work, the Hasidim embraced it. In fact, according to some scholars, it was their work ethic that, early on, helped to ensure the continued existence of the Hasidic movement.[2]

In keeping with Hasidic theology's positive view of worldly work, the Hasidic rebbes who settled in America after the war strongly encouraged their followers to go to work—despite a profound concern with minimizing their contact with the potentially corrupting secular world. While teaching in the community's fledgling yeshivas remained a viable option for some men, others were forced to acquire new skills to enable them to find jobs outside the community, as cutters or tailors in the garment trade, as cutters and polishers in the diamond industry, or as electricians, plumbers, plasterers, or painters. Younger members of the community enrolled in courses in accounting or computer programming, and some became wholesalers and retailers of electronic equipment. Those who were able to raise the money went into real estate development, manufacturing, construction, or the diamond business. All of these jobs had the advantage of requiring only limited contact with outsiders and did not, for the most part, necessitate any alteration of Hasidic styles of dress or major compromises in religious observance.[3]

Those Hasidim who were successful in business not only provided jobs for others, but also contributed large sums to create and sustain community institutions, and to support community charities. At the time, these growing communities required little financial support from the city and state to maintain their systems of education and justice; the private schools were run by the community, and charity provided enough to support the poor and sick. As had been the case for these communities before their arrival in America, most disputes were settled in rabbinical courts.

By the middle of the 1960s, however, the number of Hasidim in New York City had grown close to fifty thousand, with Satmar representing the largest sect, at 1300 families.[4] With their very high birthrates quickly driving up the population, and their paucity of educational credentials, the Hasidim had, in a sense, become the victims of their own success. In the decades that followed, Hasidic leaders began to have to look to federal, state, and local programs to aid the poor and bring resources into the community. Strenuous efforts by the community leadership—bolstered by the successful cultivation of political connections and the acquisition of technical expertise—resulted in an influx of government and private sector support for job training and commercial ventures. According to Kranzler,[5] most notable among these achievements was the official designation in 1984 of the Hasidim as a "Disadvantaged Minority," enabling them to benefit from the same programs that were available to other racial and ethnic minorities.

While these economic changes were occurring within the Hasidic community in America, the differences that had long distinguished the Hasidim from the Misnagdim were beginning to blur as well. Today, as the Hasidim have reelevated the Orthodox commitment to Talmudic study and strict observance of Jewish law, the Misnagdim, for their part, have also adopted some practices traditionally associated with Hasidism. These include the veneration of charismatic leaders and the need to associate the divine with a living representative, something that was once—and even now continues to be—one of the most important and fundamental ideological distinctions between the two groups. Indeed, it is precisely this kind of veneration that has given the Hasidim a reputation for idol worship.[6]

So, as much as Yossi liked to see the current economic situation of the Hasidic community as the result of an intentional plot devised by "evil genius" leaders of the various sects, in fact, a combination of ideological, demographic, and political factors is responsible for the high level of Hasidic poverty and dependency. No doubt, the Hasidic rejection of secular education and emphasis on large families have played a major role in Hasidic poverty and reliance on government support, but so have the government's historically liberal welfare policies—not to mention politicians' eternal willingness to court communities that are able to deliver large blocs of votes.[7] Nonetheless, Yossi still believed that by painting the secular world as such a corrupt, dangerous (and ultimately even anti-Semitic) place, and by denying people the skills to engage with it productively, the rebbes had succeeded in building their communities not so much on the strength of their philosophies, but on people's most basic fears.

In fact, while he was doing some research several years earlier, Yossi had come across an advertisement in a 1973 issue of *Der Yid*, the Satmar paper, that said it all for him. Printed in Yiddish, the ad read:

> *United Rabbis of the U.S. and Canada*
> *Strict Warning!*
> *We warn again that those who don't need it for their health should not go to Miami, or similar places, and those who do need to go, should know*

> *that the area near the ocean is*
> *Forbidden by Halakhic Law*
> *To live there or go there.*
> *And it is included in the law of "there is another way." When one has another way to go, and doesn't need to pass through the areas that might lead one to sin. And may those who heed be graced, and blessings should come upon them.*

To Yossi, this demonization of an entire city—presumably because there was mixed bathing in the ocean—was "classic Hasidic craziness." He had thought about sending the ad to the Miami board of tourism. Surely it would come as a shock to them that Jews were forbidden from visiting the place.

Of course, Yossi knew that the community also did a lot to help people, and that nobody ever went without food, a place to stay, or medical attention. Everyone was always busy collecting for people in need, at every *simcha*, or celebration, every gathering and event. Indeed, one could hardly go to any function without someone passing around a large manila envelope and asking for a contribution for this one's medical treatment or that one's new baby's layette. In some ways, this was a great part of the community's life, a kind of socialism that Yossi believed had some merit. He also thought it might be related to the fact that Jews in general tended to give so much to charity and seemed to like to help other people. Sometimes, however, he also felt that the community actually needed its poorest members in order to make the others look and feel good by giving—especially rich families that could use money to overcome their lack of yiches. And, as Yossi was beginning to understand more and more these days, all of this kindness and charity often came at a price.

When Yossi could no longer stand being cooped up like a prisoner, he began slinking out of his house and the neighborhood, in the garb, through the Italian section and over to the subway. One day on his way to the train, he couldn't resist going into a hardware store where a friend of his was a salesman. When he stepped inside, his friend approached him, asking if he needed any help. Yossi played it up for a few minutes, asking about different brands of air conditioners and fans, until his friend finally realized who he was and let out a blood-curdling scream. His reaction was so extreme—moaning and yelling about *how could he do this*, and *what, was he crazy?*—that Yossi ended up running out of the store in a panic, straight to the subway.

Usually, Yossi would catch a train heading into Manhattan, where he could disappear for a few hours into the mainstream. His first forays were to his old, familiar, pre-shave haunts: the public library on Forty-second Street, where he could read Yiddish books and newspapers, and schmooze with his librarian friend; the YIVO Institute for Jewish Research downtown; the video room at the library of the Jewish Theological Seminary up at Columbia.

The whole situation felt very strange to Yossi. He had always imagined that once he had shaved, he would be out of the garb completely, living a totally different life, filled with excitement and fun. Sometimes he thought about trying to go buy some "civilian" clothes that he could wear once he got into Manhattan, safely away from the eyes of his community. But then he would have to schlep a big bag around with him all day and find places to change. All of this could have been managed, of course; the main impediment was actually that Yossi had no money to buy anything more than subway rides and an occasional ninety-nine-cent burger at McDonald's. His portion of the small amount of money his father had left for him and his sister was already almost gone.

In between all the reading and film watching, Yossi would use the computers in the various libraries he was visiting to check out the Internet, searching for free things to do, places to go, people to meet. He registered with a Web site that listed every Jewish event in the city, and pretty soon he was receiving as many as fifteen e-mail invitations a day: Jewish singles parties everywhere from the East Village and non-Hasidic Williamsburg (hip and secular) to the Upper West Side (marriage-focused and religious); concerts featuring klezmer bands and neo-Hasidic rappers; lectures at the Workmen's Circle, a Jewish socialist organization. His most bizarre experience was an event that had the word "Lilith" in the title, and which seemed to offer the possibility of meeting women. When Yossi showed up there, however, it turned out to be a group of radical Jewish lesbians reading their poems about male oppression and the plight of the Palestinian people. Despite the puzzled stares and whispers, Yossi ended up having a good time with the lesbians, and they seemed not to mind him too much, either. He tried to hit as many of these free events as he could, mostly to avoid having to go back to his neighborhood before he could slide in under the relative cover of darkness.

One night at an experimental dance performance somewhere in downtown Manhattan, Yossi was approached by a man named Elly, who had recognized something familiar in Yossi's clothing and demeanor. It turned out that he had left a different ultra-Orthodox community many years ago. Now in his late thirties, Elly was attending evening classes at Columbia and working a number of different day jobs to pay the rent on his one-bedroom apartment in the East Village. During his free time, he was also learning to play the guitar and writing poetry, while trying, albeit as yet unsuccessfully, to find himself a girlfriend. Elly's relations with his family were strained, to say the least; he hadn't seen any of them, except for one brother, in close to three years. It was very painful, but he was dealing with the stress.

That night, Elly gave Yossi his phone number and told him that there were others out there like him, a small group of men, and even a few women, who were a little older and who had broken away from their religious communities some time ago. They would probably be happy to talk to him, if Yossi was interested. Elly mentioned that he had even heard of a young Lubavitcher woman named Malkie Schwartz, who had left that community several years ago and was now thinking about trying to help others who wanted to do the same. Elly didn't know her personally and wasn't sure how she could be contacted, but there was also Chaim, an unmarried Hasidic man in his mid-forties who was actually religious, but very open. Chaim had a place on the outskirts of a Hasidic community in Brooklyn—a hangout where all sorts of people came and went all the time. It was very *heimish*, and nobody judged anyone else. Elly gave Yossi Chaim's number and the address of his place. He assured Yossi that he would be welcome there.

This was exciting news. But as much as Yossi had longed to find others who were in his position, something about meeting Elly had made him feel a little uncomfortable. Certainly, he liked the idea that there were people who knew where he was coming from and who might be able to help him find his way in the outside world a little. But he also felt that he hadn't gone to all this trouble to end up hanging out with a bunch of guys who were just like he was, even though he knew they would have a lot in common. What if it turned out that they were actually just as much a closed group as the one he was trying to flee? Yossi also had to admit to himself that Elly's life sounded considerably less glamorous than he had imagined his own life would be, once he broke free. Truthfully, he was also really much more interested in meeting girls anyway. Maybe this Malkie Schwartz would be someone to try to find.

But Yossi did like the sound of Chaim and his hangout. A quick subway ride could take him there easily, and maybe it wouldn't hurt to check the place out a little. The only thing that concerned Yossi was whether Elly was exaggerating. What if it turned out that Chaim wasn't so nonjudgmental after all? If he was still religious, how could he be so open? Yossi certainly didn't feel ready to expose himself to more badgering, or to having to justify and account for himself—at least not just yet. So, after bidding Elly goodbye, Yossi folded up the piece of paper he had given him and shoved it into his pocket. He wanted a little more time to float around before settling on his next move.

Chapter Four

From the Outskirts

In a barren garden behind a run-down tenement on the outskirts of Boro Park, several men in Hasidic garb are arranging hot dogs, corn, and chicken wings on a kosher charcoal grill. The plaintive sound of the Muslim call to prayer from the mosque down the street has been drowned out by The Gypsy Kings' version of "Hotel California," blasting from a boom box that sits on a nearby table, next to tins of Spanish rice, "Southern" vegetarian cholent (a modified version of a classic Eastern European Jewish dish), and bottles of ketchup, mustard, and Pepsi. One of the men—overweight, with suspenders and a big, dark beard—is opining on the recent, untimely death of a 1980s pop star. "I loved her songs because they were so much about longing and disappointment, both things that are to me deeply familiar," he says in his thick Yiddish accent, to no one in particular.

As the food grills, more people make their way down a dirt path from the side street: groups of men in Hasidic "summer" dress (black pants, white shirts, black velvet kippahs, *tzitzit*, and peyos, but no coats or hats), and others in more contemporary attire (shorts, jeans, khakis). Some of these more "modern" types sport beards and baseball caps, while others are clean-shaven, their heads uncovered. By the end of the night, close to fifty people will fill the small patch of dirt, almost all men, of varying ages and religious commitments, some not even Jewish. (A subsequent night here will include a Korean cyclist who heard about the place via an e-mail on his BlackBerry from a friend in Japan, and decided to stop by for a hot meal before resuming his around-the-world bike tour.)

This barbecue is one of many that Chaim hosts throughout the summer. Those in attendance make up a motley crew of Chaim's friends, acquaintances, and friends of friends, all of whom receive the invitation by phone call, word of mouth, or e-mail. While these outdoor gatherings have become a staple of the summer months, Chaim maintains an office space in the building that abuts the garden, where people are welcome all year long, anytime, day or night. In this ramshackle three-room apartment with sloping floors, peeling paint, a few desks, two worn couches, stacks of bulging boxes, an Internet connection, and no readily identifiable signs of industry, the group can hang out and eat pretzels, fruit, and fireball candies; drink iced tea, soda, vodka, or schnapps; strum an old guitar; surf the Net; read books and magazines; and discuss and debate whatever happens to be on their minds.

Tonight, while two guys over by the cholent are considering the possibly Arabic derivation of the name "Ferengi" (an alien race on *Star Trek* with suspiciously stereotypical medieval Jewish traits, according to some aficionados), Chaim and one of his other friends are enlightening me on the implications of the differences between ancient Greek and Jewish law pertaining to slave ownership. The two also tell me that they are hatching a plan to sponsor an informal lecture series, to take place upstairs in the office in the fall. The series will include volunteer speakers sharing their expertise on various aspects of Hasidic philosophy. Chaim jokes that he might even be able to entice Madonna, with her newfound interest in Kabbalah, to take part in the proceedings. Maybe she would learn something.

With the addition of a TV and constant talk of sports and women, this place might seem like any local bar or social club, except that many of its "regulars" were raised and continue to live in Hasidic communities, where watching *Star Trek*—let alone discussing it while listening to The Gypsy Kings and mixing freely with women and the nonreligious—would surely mark a man as a lowlife to be both pitied and shunned. Indeed, it strikes me that in form and atmosphere, if not exactly in content, this place might not be so far from the chaotic religious study halls where Hasidic men learn in pairs or groups, debating points of Jewish law in between downing cups of coffee, smoking cigarettes, and exchanging community gossip.

Many of the people who come here are Hasidic men who are misfits in the sense that they just can't fit into the life the community demands of them. Some are looking for more freedom but, with wives and children, feel they cannot leave the community. Others, particularly the older ones, a few of whom are divorced, claim that they don't see any need to leave; generally comfortable with their lives and fearful of starting anew at their age, these people nonetheless long for more intellectual freedom and a broader range of life experiences and personal relationships than the community currently permits. For both types, Chaim's space offers the opportunity to be with like-minded, familiar people, providing camaraderie and some room to breathe.

There are also people here who have left the community (and in some cases also the religion), but who want, or even need, to maintain some sort of positive connection to their native world. Often, they find themselves seated next to someone seeking encouragement for his or her own process of *becoming* religious. Chaim, with his gentle manner and sly wit, his long, spindly beard, and the peyos coiled up tightly and tucked behind his ears, seems to welcome them all.

In fact, Chaim, who is himself strictly observant, has been playing host to such types, informally and in various discreet locations, for close to twenty years, encompassing two generations. He is not sure exactly how many people out there might be disaffected or questioning, how many are still appearing publicly in Hasidic garb but are no longer observant. The informal estimate he and his friend Teddy (himself an ex-Hasid who has known Chaim since these informal gatherings began) give me is around five hundred, but both emphasize that this number is largely impressionistic, that there could be more.

Chaim believes that he is personally acquainted with somewhere between fifty and one hundred of these types, a group that doesn't include what the Orthodox community has come to call "kids at risk"—a phenomenon of growing concern, increasingly addressed in the Jewish media.[1] Indeed, a study carried out in 1999 found that there were 1500 young people between the ages of eleven and twenty in the Orthodox communities of Brooklyn engaged in serious at-risk behavior.[2] According to the study, this included anything from aggressive behavior to vandalism, theft, credit card fraud, substance abuse, addiction, drug dealing, promiscuous sexual activity, and the public flouting of communal rules and norms. The study also estimated that another two thousand young people were doing the same things, but had yet to be caught. If the numbers were accurate, that would have amounted to about 3.75 percent of the Brooklyn Orthodox teen population.[3]

Chaim claims that he has no agenda but to give people a place to relax and "chill out" without feeling marginalized or judged—particularly those who are without a clear social role in the community, such as divorced or older single people. However, he does allow that he wants those who are questioning their beliefs to be able to address their religious concerns in an environment that is removed from what he sees as the "community craziness"—namely, the obsession with image and appearance rather than substance and meaning. According to Chaim, *es past nisht*—which roughly translates to "that's inappropriate"—is an all too commonly used phrase in Hasidic homes. If people were more familiar with both the history and the texts, if they had a more sophisticated understanding, Chaim believes, they wouldn't "fetishize" the clothing so much, or get so worked up about being contaminated by the outside world. Of course, Chaim acknowledges that there are some people whose experiences in the community have been so painful—they may have been molested, or severely emotionally abused—that the religion has been irrevocably tainted for them as well.

Chaim believes that most of the younger people in the community today have been raised on a steady diet of fear, fed to them both at home and at school, and that, despite the putative emphasis on learning, the average young Hasid remains profoundly ignorant of Hasidic philosophy and Jewish history. If only people could separate the religion from the community, Chaim is sure that there would be a lot less disaffection than he currently sees, although he concedes that making this distinction in one's mind doesn't make it so in real life. After all, no matter how much they come to appreciate the myriad insights of Judaism and the beauty of Hasidic thought and practice, these people still have to live in the community. And unless someone starts a revolution, things don't seem likely to change dramatically anytime soon. Chaim certainly doesn't see himself as a revolutionary, however. While he is not interested in convincing other people to live as he does, Chaim's commitment to Judaism is such that he nonetheless feels a profound sadness whenever a person who grew up Hasidic makes the decision to completely abandon the tradition.

For Chaim, if someone comes to the conclusion that he or she does not believe and wants to stop observing, so be it—provided that this decision has been reached through a sincere process of genuine struggle, not merely as a result of "immature rebellion" (characterized by the predictable trifecta of excessive drinking, drug use, and promiscuity). Maybe such a person will at least maintain the connection in other ways: by eating traditional foods and celebrating certain holidays (every year Chaim hosts a blow-out Purim party, where people have been known to come dressed as Jesus, or in drag, and a guest once drank so much he had to be carted off on a Hatzolah stretcher); by engaging with Jewish texts or learning about Jewish history; by taking seriously the Jewish obligation to "repair the world" *(tikkun olam)*.

This hope might go some way toward explaining why Chaim never objected when one of his former employees, a married Hasid who was struggling with his sexual identity, decided to wear a dress, makeup, and a long wig around the office. Perhaps Chaim felt that the acceptance of his religious coworkers might decrease the likelihood that this man would feel the need to reject his background altogether. Or maybe Chaim and the others just liked his outfit. Chaim is an ultra-Orthodox man whose attitude is clearly far from orthodox. Despite his unwavering commitment to his religion, his attitudes and behavior leave no doubt that Chaim is operating on the margins of the contemporary Hasidic world. While he considers himself a true Hasid, the mainstream of the community would most certainly see him as a heretic.

Chaim's commitment to Judaism, and Hasidism in particular, does not exactly mean that he is an unquestioning believer, however. It's more that he grew up at a time when the community was not as insular and restrictive as it is these days. His was a loving family with parents who let him read all kinds of books, watch television, and even raise pet chickens in his back yard—all things he claims would be unheard of in most Hasidic households today. While the Hasidic understanding of God's presence in the physical world encourages a respect for animals and nature, in practice, the Hasidim tend not to have pets. Some scholars claim that this is because Jews are an urban people, unused to living among animals. Others maintain that, because certain animals—like dogs—were not sacrificed in Jerusalem's holy temple, Jews should not bring them, or any other nonkosher animal, into their homes. Indeed, many Hasidim are afraid of dogs, which saddens Chaim.

Unlike many people he knows, Chaim has always experienced religion as something positive, linking him to the history of a great people and their rich traditions, and giving him a sense of how he fits into a larger scheme. Despite all of this, Chaim admits that, were he a betting man, he would probably bet that the Torah was not divinely revealed to Moses at Sinai, and that God doesn't really care about whether he carries out all of the commandments. (Like most of the men here, he also laughs uproariously at the community's position that dinosaurs are the creation of modern propagandists, otherwise known as scientists.) In fact, Chaim admits that, were he a betting man, he would likely bet against the existence of God altogether—but he isn't a betting man.

—

Chaim's views seem remarkable to me, as does the confidence with which he expresses them and puts them into practice. My guess is that not having a wife and a house full of children (also remarkable, in this community) might have something to do with his self-proclaimed comfort with his life. Unlike the majority of Hasidic people, not only has he had plenty of time to grow up, but he also continues to enjoy a degree of freedom unknown to most Hasidic adults, particularly women. Chaim knows many Hasidim who, having married at nineteen and had children soon after, later came to realize that they had never had time for exploration, for adolescence. This can cause something like a midlife crisis—except that, in this case, the crisis happens at the age of twenty-eight or twenty-nine.

So why, I ask Chaim tonight, given his doubts about God, does he remain strictly observant? Why not, for instance, become a Reform Jew? This question prompts a response I will end up hearing from Hasidic people—whether religious or lapsed—over and over again. Growing up Orthodox, he explains, makes any other form of observance feel watered-down, compromised. Orthodox Jews live their lives according to their religious beliefs, while other types of Jews make their beliefs conform to their lifestyles. And even though Chaim, ever the nonbetting man, doesn't necessarily believe, he thinks it would be frivolous to abandon the practices his great-grandparents died trying to preserve, all for the sake of the taste of a ham sandwich. These practices, given how things are going, could soon disappear altogether.

Fair enough—although I tell him I am quite certain that nobody ever gives up a religion merely for the taste of a ham sandwich, and that he knows it, too. The "rebellious" kids who want to experiment with drugs and sex often have other issues, and a great majority of them eventually come back. But, if wanting more freedom is such a big concern for the people who come to Chaim's place, why, I ask, don't some of them just become what is known as modern Orthodox? This would allow them to engage with the secular world, go to college, and enter the professions, while remaining strictly observant. From the look on Chaim's face, it is as if I have asked him to put his pet chickens on the grill and serve them to his guests.

The pop music fan in suspenders comes quickly to Chaim's rescue. It turns out his name is Avi, and that he is divorced, in his late forties. Despite his heavily accented English, Avi has been able to make himself a very good living in the printing business.

"Modern Orthodox Jews are fakers," Avi tells me, moving his hands in the air as if he is brushing lint off an invisible man's suit. "They want for it to be both ways," he continues with a big shrug. "To be modern and traditional at the same time. But it cannot work. They just end up bringing all of their cold, modern rationality to their performance of the mitzvot." Considering that there is no serious dispute between the modern Orthodox and the Hasidim on matters of Jewish law, Avi's emotional reaction must be coming from another place.

"Among these modern Orthodox, there is no *feeling*, no *heart*, no *fire*," Avi explains. Apparently, the modern Orthodox are an altogether different breed from the Hasidim, the *real* Orthodox, who wear exotic outfits and sing and dance, and actually do tremble before God, who tell rebbe stories and colorful Yiddish jokes, and who live in a *real* community, where people do for each other. For Avi at least, the modern types are so busy with their laws that they have no culture. Of course, it is also worth noting that the modern Orthodox pose the greatest threat to strictly Orthodox Jews, passively challenging them to consider that perhaps one can live a "Torah life" and still engage with the modern, secular world.

Suddenly, I realize that Avi is sounding very much the way I imagine the original Hasidim might have sounded, when, in their attempt to revive a beleaguered Eastern European Jewry, they rejected the spiritually bereft and legalistic Judaism they had inherited, in favor of one that emphasized ecstatic prayer, charismatic leadership, egalitarianism, and pageantry. It is indeed tempting to view Chaim and his friends as closer than the rest of their community to the original Hasidim, although their doubts about divine revelation and the existence of God ultimately place them squarely in a more modern, "enlightened" camp. It is hard to be ecstatically devoted to God if one is not even sure whether He exists. Nonetheless, it does indeed seem ironic, though hardly surprising, that much of what the Hasidic movement originally sought to critique has now been incorporated into it; after all, charismatic leadership and egalitarian social structures and practices are difficult to sustain over time.

"And talk about making religion fit your lifestyle," Avi says, startling me out of my own thoughts. Evidently, it is currently popular among the modern Orthodox to have what they call "*tefillin* dates," meaning that, when a man goes out at night with a woman, he brings his tefillin (the leather phylacteries men bind to their arms during prayer) with him, so as to have them the next day, when he says his morning prayers. "Who has heard of such a thing? A Jewish man doesn't sleep with a Jewish woman before they are married."

I sense an opening, and a possible change of course. "But what if the woman isn't Jewish?" I ask, already aware of what the answer might be, from having heard several other men address this question. This is another story, he explains, a twinkle in his eye. As long as the man is not planning to marry the non-Jewish woman, this is OK, not serious. After all, Avi assures me, men are not like women. They have needs, urges, like animals, he explains. Even the rabbis understood this. If a man's wife is unable to take care of those needs (as is the case when she is menstruating), or if he is divorced or widowed, he is permitted to get his needs satisfied elsewhere.[4] As long, of course, as the woman is not Jewish. If she is, it's much more problematic. If not, the wife will understand.

She will?

It seems to me that this might be the right time to ask Chaim and Avi why there are so few women here tonight, and apparently none at all from the community (there are two women here who took the subway in from Manhattan, both of whom are in the process of becoming Orthodox). The two men stop to think. Chaim offers that maybe women in general are happier in the community than men are and, as a result, have less desire to transgress than the men do. Or, perhaps the community's discouragement of female religious scholarship makes women less intellectually curious in general, and thus less likely to want to explore the world beyond the community's borders. Isn't it always the case in traditional societies that the women hold on more tightly to tradition than the men? Chaim suggests.

Avi claims that many Hasidic women have turned their brains off completely, focusing instead on cooking and cleaning and diapering and shopping. It's not that they don't have intelligence, these women, but just that they don't know how to *think*. In fact, it was only when he took an accounting class outside of the community and, for the first time in his life, befriended women that Avi realized they could in fact be as intellectually oriented as men. It was also through that class that he realized he very much enjoyed the company of these women, taking them out to dinner and hoping that one might even become his girlfriend. As a divorced older man in the community, he gets only the dregs from the matchmakers, people with deformities or mental illnesses. Or those notoriously unstable baalei teshuvah whose lack of background often blinds them to the nuances of community life and who, with the zeal of the newly converted, can be even more fanatic than the most religious Hasid born into the community.

Avi admits that he desperately wants to experience a little romance, although of course he would never consider marrying one of the women from his class, or even bringing her anywhere near the community. Then he could never expect to get a match, and of course his children would suffer irreparably as well. One has to be discreet. However, he would like to stop having to visit "professionals," if I know what he means, even though he assures me that he treats them with the utmost respect, and tips them well, as he believes all of their Hasidic patrons do.

I cannot hold back any longer. Forget the prostitutes for now. Might the dearth of women here tonight have something to do with the fact that, in the Hasidic community, women have the primary responsibility for the home and children? I ask Avi. Maybe the demands of this role allow women comparatively little time and opportunity even to contemplate expanding their horizons, let alone to act on such an idea. Is it possible that not all of the women are thrilled to be diapering and cooking, but that they have to do these things if the family is to function smoothly? Perhaps what Avi interprets as not thinking merely reflects the fact that women are kept from learning most of the things that men do, and, as a result, haven't been trained to think about the same things, or in the same ways, that men have?

The two stop to consider my apparently novel hypotheses. Could be, they say, shaking their heads. Could be. It's hard to know for sure, Chaim says, because there really is very little occasion for men to get to know women in the community, and vice versa. But Chaim really believes that the main reason almost no women come here is that the men probably wouldn't like it too much. After all, many of them hang out here to get some time *away* from their wives. And, while they might well be interested in socializing with other men's wives, this could, of course, become dangerous. People might flirt. Things could get out of hand. He isn't ready to shake up the whole system, after all.

In the end, it seems that this place functions mostly as a kind of safety valve, relieving pressure building up in the system, and in the lives of individuals, without actually changing much of anything. For some of the group, this likely works very well, making difficult lives more bearable, or "multiple" lives more possible. Interestingly, though, I haven't met anyone here like Steinmetz, the bibliophile, or P., the apikoros. In fact, neither of them would come anywhere near this place, and not because they wouldn't like everyone here, or wouldn't have all sorts of things to discuss with them. It's just that Steinmetz would be far too scared of discovery, and P. would find it depressing, like a ghetto within a ghetto. And he, too, certainly wouldn't want to risk his reputation, precisely because, so far at least, he has managed his double life so well.

There is little doubt that people like Avi and Chaim would be happy to welcome Steinmetz and P., would keep their secrets, and would probably even try to get Steinmetz to give a talk for the upcoming lecture series. But this is not going to happen. What is true for most of the Hasidim here tonight is also true for Steinmetz and P. and so many others: Keeping up appearances and avoiding exposure in the community is preferable to sacrificing their livelihoods and threatening their children's welfare. And it's also much less stressful than undertaking a radical shift in their way of life that could sever their ties to family and friends. For these people, all things considered, it is much easier to straddle two worlds than to be forced to live in only one.

As I bite into a perfectly grilled ear of corn, I think about what becomes of those people who can't or won't live in two worlds. People who don't feel content to maintain double lives and keep up appearances, no matter what the consequences. People, for example, like Malkie Schwartz.

Chapter Five

Coming and Going

Even with the big fur *shtreimel* on his head, Yossi was freezing his tuchus off, standing on the corner of Varick and Canal in lower Manhattan. It was an unseasonably cold early November day, and a bitter wind swept up the street from the river, blowing his bekishe up around his legs till he felt like some kind of Hasidic version of Marilyn Monroe on the subway grate. Yossi needed a drink; he was still nervous and a bit shaky after his narrow escape from the "'chood," as they liked to call it in "Hebonics." It was a daring move, taking the subway out of the community on Shabbos, but walking the long, ice-cold blocks to the Church Avenue subway stop had paid off; there hadn't been another Hasid in sight.

Yossi looked around, trying to get his bearings. He had switched trains so many times to get here that he wasn't exactly sure where he was, but the guy from the bar had insisted that the massage parlor was only half a block from this subway stop. Still, Yossi didn't see anything that looked as if it could be the place, though he imagined they probably didn't have a big flashing neon sign over the door, either. There was a skinny, strung-out looking black woman huddled in the entryway of a nearby deli, and, for a minute, Yossi thought about offering her ten bucks for a quick *shtup*. She didn't look as if she would mind the offer. And he was getting desperate.

Even so, Yossi felt good to be in Manhattan, despite the bitter cold. In fact, this was the only time in his life that he could remember being so thankful that he had a beard; it was keeping the lower half of his face from going completely numb. And getting out of Brooklyn, especially on a Saturday—when a Hasid couldn't do anything much but pray and eat and read and sleep, waiting endlessly for darkness to come—was well worth the physical discomfort. Emotionally, life had been pretty hard for Yossi for the last few months, ever since the day his father had found out about the shave.

The news first made it up to the mountains through a neighbor who had spotted Yossi on the street rushing off to the subway and immediately called to alert his father, up in the bungalow colony. That night, Yossi's father had called him at home in Brooklyn, and when Yossi picked up the phone, his father's first reaction was one of shock: Why was it that Yossi sounded exactly the same as he always did when he'd had the beard? How could this possibly be? his father wanted to know. He had expected to hear the voice of a total lunatic on the other end of the line, because only a person who had completely lost his mind would even think of doing something as crazy as this. Yossi quietly reminded his father that he had shaved off only his beard, not his personality. There was no reason to think he would sound any different than he always had. He wasn't crazy.

If he wasn't crazy, then what could be the explanation for this? his father demanded. Yossi had sinned against God by his actions, and he had upset his mother and brothers terribly. Couldn't he hear them all sobbing in the background? How would his brothers and sisters ever get decent shidduchim now? Maybe if Yossi let the beard and peyos grow back, maybe then people might forget about this, dismiss it as some kind of silly rebellion, just a phase. Things might be all right, if he did that. Yossi could wear a shorter suit and a more modern, "bent down" hat, if he preferred that look. That would be OK. It wasn't what his father had in mind for him, but it would do, if it had to. Then maybe at least he could get some tutoring jobs again, perhaps teaching the children of baalei teshuvah, who might not know enough to care about this lapse. Maybe things would be all right if he just sat at home and let his beard grow back.

Yossi listened to his father, as he always did, and then tried calmly to tell him that his beard was his own business and that he wasn't planning to grow it back, or to wear a shorter suit, or any suit, for that matter. This life just wasn't for him anymore. Couldn't they agree to disagree?

His father's voice quickly grew louder and much, much angrier. Why did Yossi want to become a *shaigetz?* He was aware that Yossi went to the library to read books sometimes. Maybe they had poisoned his mind, filled it with bad thoughts and silly ideas. That was it. He was sick from all of the garbage he had been dumping into his head, his father declared, his voice temporarily brightening from the hope of a cure. Maybe he needed to see a doctor for some pills that would fix his obviously diseased mind. Or perhaps, he changed tack, this all came about because he had not been praying enough. Was he putting on tefillin every day? And going to shul to *daven*, or to the beis medrash to learn? This would surely help return him to God and to the truth, to what was right and good and holy and pure.

Yossi could not even begin to imagine what his father would say or do if he knew that Yossi never put on tefillin anymore, that he hadn't been keeping kosher, and had been secretly violating the Sabbath pretty much ever since his divorce. Cutting off the beard and peyos had been the last step, not the first.

When it became clear to his father that Yossi had nothing more to say, he began an all too familiar rant that Yossi had heard at home and in school and in the larger community for as long as he could remember: Yossi was worse than Hitler. Didn't he see that shaving his beard was like killing his Jewish identity? He was carrying out Hitler's work, destroying himself and, with him, the whole of the Jewish people. And he was a Jew! Yossi was a Nazi and a murderer, and his father ordered him to pack up his clothes and get out of the house *right now*. His younger brothers and sisters could not come home and be exposed to such a terrible influence. What he had done was a *shonda*, a disgrace. And why should his siblings have to pay for Yossi's sins with bad matches?

A Nazi? A murderer? Yossi knew that being called these names was supposed to make him feel guilty, to convince him of the error of his ways. It was supposed to make him change his mind and grow back his beard and start praying three times a day, as he had been taught and had done since he was boy. But the only thing Yossi felt was rage. All his life he hadn't made trouble for anyone. He had studied hard and been an excellent learner, earning all A's in yeshiva and great praise from his teachers. He had never gotten involved with drugs, or stolen anything from anyone, like some of the more rebellious boys. And he had even married a girl he had known was wrong for him from the start, just to get everyone off his back, and also to allow his next youngest sister to get started on finding a husband for herself. Yossi could hardly manage to raise his voice at another person, even when he wanted to. And now, all of a sudden, he was Hitler.

Yossi had heard and seen this tactic used on people many times before, even in small ways. In school, when kids ran around and misbehaved, the teachers would yell at them, declaring that they were obviously not good little Jewish boys but evil Gestapo soldiers. And if anyone—even a Jew—said something people didn't like about the community, that person was also "a Nazi." Why was everyone still so busy with Hitler, Yossi had long wondered. Didn't he already do enough harm?

Thankfully, Yossi's grandmother agreed to take him in after his father ordered him to leave their apartment. Maybe, Yossi reasoned, his father had known this would happen and wouldn't have kicked him out without the safety net of his grandmother. Yossi couldn't be sure of this, however, given how angry his father had been. But it was OK with Yossi. His grandmother's house was large and clean and comfortable, nothing like the cramped, run-down, one-bathroom railroad flat he had shared with the ten other people in his family. His younger siblings never gave him any peace there anyway. And his grandmother was very nice to him, buying the foods that he liked and letting him watch TV in a room with the door closed, as long as the volume wasn't up too loud.

Sometimes late at night Yossi and his grandmother would talk, and he would ask her about her life and whether she was happy with the way everything had turned out for her. She told him that, for the most part, she was content with her life. Her husband had been a good provider, and she had always loved him, even if she never really understood why he had become so extreme with the religion. Of course, she missed some of her old friends and relatives who had become more secular, and the ones who had died. She also missed doing things like going out to the movies or to Manhattan for a show, although she was too busy with her family to bother with any of that now. And even though this craziness of having so many children was beyond her, she couldn't help but feel proud that her marriage alone had resulted in close to seventy offspring, of three generations. Everyone in the family seemed to be healthy, thank God, and nobody had a problem with drugs or crime, like so many other young people today. For this, she told Yossi, she felt blessed.

Yossi had the sense that, on some level, his grandmother really understood him, even though she never actually told him she approved of what he had done, getting rid of the beard and the peyos. She showed her support in other ways, by giving him a little money each week, and trying to find someone who might hire him, a relative of a friend, or a neighbor's son, even for a menial job, so that he would at least have some money and some structure. And when Yossi disappeared on Shabbos, as he had been doing more and more, she never bothered to ask him in too much detail where he had been or what he had done. Sometimes she even borrowed the books he brought home from the flea market in Manhattan.

About a month after Yossi had begun living with his grandmother, his father managed to arrange some tutoring work for him. With no other prospects, Yossi felt he had no choice, and began meeting with several boys a few times a week to teach them religious subjects. As his father had predicted, they were the children of baalei teshuvah, living nearby, though in a more liberal, less insular community. While Yossi's background as a Hasid made him attractive to the parents as a tutor for their children (he actually knew more than they could ever teach their kids), the parents' backgrounds made them a little more lenient and less judgmental than anyone in Yossi's own community would have been. They didn't seem to care or even really notice that he had a short (only half-grown) beard. This was a big relief to Yossi, as even some of his closest friends had stopped inviting him over for Shabbos, or just to hang out and schmooze at night. They would still talk to him on the phone, or agree to meet him somewhere on the outskirts of the community, but they didn't dare risk having him in their homes, exposing their children to him. They all claimed their wives wouldn't let them.

Yossi knew that his father had arranged these jobs in order to prevent him from going completely off the path, which he was still terrified Yossi would do. He knew that Yossi needed the money, and the act of teaching a boy Talmud might bring him back to the beauty of learning as well. Also, even though the parents were baalei teshuvah, Yossi still had to come to the sessions wearing at least a kippah. After all, these boys' parents were paying Yossi not only for his knowledge, but also for his example.

The arrangement had been working out pretty well, but Yossi sometimes became depressed; he felt like a hypocrite, teaching these boys things that he himself no longer believed. And sitting there with them day after day couldn't help but remind him of how confined he had felt doing the same thing for so many years. And he couldn't share any of this with the boys, of course. The whole situation made him feel very isolated and alone. Maybe all of this had something to do with Yossi's decision to take the bartender's advice and cut out of the neighborhood on this particular Saturday, in search of a massage and a "Happy Ending."

Yossi walked a few blocks to the north and then back around and south, but still he couldn't find the massage parlor. He wanted to call the bartender, but he didn't have his number. He figured that if worse came to worst, he could pick up a copy of the *Village Voice*, where there were always pages and pages of listings for call girls and escort services—although he had been told that they often charged a hefty price. The *Bay News*, a local paper in Brooklyn, certainly offered cheaper deals closer to home—he had sampled their wares a few times in the past few months—but he didn't have a copy with him and had no idea where in Manhattan he might get one.

As Yossi was weighing his options, he suddenly noticed something that looked promising to the east, down Canal Street. It was next door to a luggage store, a detail the bartender had given him and that he had forgotten until this moment. That had to be the place. Yossi quickened his pace. The wind started to feel invigorating against his face.

The small room was dark and clean enough, with a red light and some soft music coming from a portable CD player in the corner. The Asian woman who was massaging him barely spoke any English, so conversation was pretty much out of the question. Yossi was surprised that he wanted to talk at all, but he did. This way, the whole thing seemed so impersonal, not unlike the times he had been intimate with his wife, climbing from his own twin bed into hers to have sex, as they had been taught. In fact, ever since Yossi had started to watch videos, he had begun to see the whole Hasidic system in a different light. Those big double beds in the movies looked so comfortable. And it seemed much nicer to be able to sleep right next to your wife, even if you weren't doing anything but sleeping.

Yossi knew that most Hasidic women used colored sheets on their bed when they weren't in niddah, switching them to white when they had their periods. People used white sheets because they were supposed to show bloodstains better. They also served to alert women's husbands that this was a time when they were barred from entering their wives' beds. In Yossi's house, after his mother would come home from the mikvah, she would immediately change the white sheets back to colored ones, and from the commotion, Yossi knew that his parents would be having sex that night. Usually, he could also tell because they would close their door for a few minutes, after which Yossi's father would emerge to wash his hands, something a man was supposed to do after sex.

After about twenty minutes of massage, the Asian woman asked

Yossi whether he "wanted Happy Ending, where I massage down there." Without giving it any thought, Yossi said yes.

The whole thing was over very fast. The woman had used some kind of oil that got hot when she rubbed it into his skin, and that also smelled a lot like watermelon bubble gum. When he was done, the woman handed Yossi a towel and told him he could get dressed. She left the room and closed the door behind her. Yossi quickly got up and dressed.

Back out on the street, Yossi suddenly felt like crying. The massage had made him feel good for a little while, but there had been no connection with the woman. It was almost as if he had been alone in that room. Suddenly, the giddy excitement of being out in Manhattan on a Saturday night had mutated into an all-enveloping sadness. The frigid wind only made the feeling worse. Yossi thought about getting back on the train and heading back to Brooklyn. He would surely be able to find some people to hang out with after Shabbos. But he didn't really want to be back there, on the streets, seeing all the people and feeling bad about himself for what he had done and what he wanted to do. He was very, very confused.

Yossi still had a few dollars left in his pocket, but not enough to do much more than get a beer at some working-class Irish bar, or a couple of ninety-nine-cent burgers at McDonalds. He started to think about tomorrow, the beginning of another week—in the Hasidic community, Sunday is like Monday—when he would have to tutor the boys. And he also thought about his failure to get on with his life and his big plans. He couldn't figure out what to do. But then suddenly he remembered that he had been carrying around Elly's number in his wallet ever since the two had met at that experimental dance performance over the summer. Maybe now was as good a time as any to give him a call. Maybe he would be able to help.

Yossi reached into his pocket and scrounged around for a quarter. He couldn't find one, so he ducked into the deli where the black woman was still huddled in the doorway. Yossi bought himself a pack of gum and got some change. As he walked out of the deli, he handed the black woman a dollar bill.

Elly picked up his cell phone after just one ring. Yossi greeted him excitedly, reminded him of who he was, and asked him whether he might be free right now to meet and talk somewhere, anywhere, his choice. It turned out, however, that Elly was in a restaurant, waiting for his date to show up. It was a first date, and he was nervous, but also pretty excited. He had met the woman online, and her picture was really cute. They had already exchanged a few good e-mails. Maybe she would finally be The One. Could he call Yossi back tomorrow?

Although he tried not to let it show in his voice, Yossi was crestfallen. He didn't want Elly to think he was a big loser. No problem, he told Elly. Tomorrow would be great. Yossi wished him *mazel* with his date and moved to hang up the phone. But before he could, he heard Elly telling him to wait. He had finally met Malkie Schwartz not too long ago, and he had her number on him, if Yossi wanted it. She seemed like a very cool person, Elly said, and she had been working to get that organization started, the one to help people like Yossi, people who wanted to explore the outside world. Maybe he should try to call her, maybe even now. She might have time to talk to him.

Suddenly, Yossi got a whiff of the watermelon massage oil wafting up from under his coat. The smell was so sickly sweet it almost nauseated him. But, as he walked away from the phone booth repeating Malkie Schwartz's number to himself over and over again so he would remember it until he got hold of another quarter, he felt the sadness begin to lift.

Chapter Six

Building a Different Kind of Chabad House

Lately, Malkie Schwartz has been spending a lot of her time at Starbucks. Unlike many New Yorkers who frequent the chain, she doesn't go there because she particularly likes coffee, or feels that she needs more light, air, and human contact than her claustrophobic apartment allows. Mainly, Malkie has been hanging out at Starbucks because its ubiquity, long hours, kosher-certified beverages, and complete indifference toward lingerers all make it the perfect place to meet with people seeking her advice and support as they begin to explore the world beyond their ultra-Orthodox[1] communities. Indeed, so much has Malkie come to regard Starbucks as a kind of office that it was at one of their locations on the Upper West Side that she suggested we first meet as well.

When I first spotted Malkie that day, it was almost impossible for me to connect her in any way to the women I had met at Suri's home, or to others I had begun to get to know in the various Hasidic communities I had been visiting. In her jeans and pink V-neck sweatshirt, dark curly hair gathered loosely in a ponytail, Malkie, at twenty-two, looked more like the college student she was than the serious and devout Hasidic girl she had so recently been. But, as I would come to appreciate again and again, clothing can do just as much to obscure as it can to reveal the person beneath it.

The oldest of nine children, Malkie was born and raised in the Lubavitcher community of Crown Heights, in Brooklyn. Neither of her parents had grown up in observant homes, but both became attracted to Lubavitch in their twenties and were introduced to the Hasidic sect—and to each other—in the mid 1970s, through the growing numbers of outreach workers who had heeded the seventh Lubavitcher rebbe's[2] call to bring Judaism to the unaffiliated. These outreach workers, known as *shluchim*, were encouraged to set up "Chabad"[3] houses (usually through their own fundraising efforts) anywhere Jews were found, and before long Lubavitchers were appearing not only on American college campuses across the country, but throughout Europe, Israel, and even Russia after the breakup of the former Soviet Union.

Today, Lubavitchers make their homes in places as far-flung, for example, as Argentina, Morocco, and South Africa. And, while Crown Heights remains the central "headquarters" of the community, Lubavitch's commitment to emissary work means that its organizational structure is necessarily more decentralized than that of the other Hasidic sects, whose members tend to live within certain physical boundaries, close to their *rebbes* and community institutions. As a result, Lubavitcher outposts are rarely as insular and tight-knit as is the community in Crown Heights.

As it has since its inception, Lubavitch outreach involves teaching Jews about their heritage,[4] setting up local congregations, and bringing kosher food to and building mikvahs in the communities where shluchim settle. A central goal of Lubavitch emissaries is to increase performance of the mitzvot (commandments) among all Jews, which, the rebbe taught, would expedite the arrival of the Messiah. In accordance with this aim, he instituted special campaigns to encourage Jewish men to put on tefillin and Jewish women to light Shabbos candles.

Despite their tireless efforts, most shluchim realize that they are unlikely to succeed in convincing others to adopt their strictly Orthodox, Lubavitch way of life. This apparently does not deter them from trying, and indeed their openness to all Jews—in addition to their use of English, more modern styles of dress, and familiarity with the outside world and secular culture—seems to make Lubavitch an attractive, nonthreatening option for many Jewish people who are seeking a deeper involvement with the religion.

Early on, the Lubavitch emphasis on outreach simultaneously benefited from and helped to foster a broader trend among previously nonreligious Jews toward increased interest in observant Judaism. This larger movement, which came to be known as "Jewish Return," began in the 1960s. Many who became involved in it were young people influenced at least in part by the countercultural climate of the times, "seekers" drawn to an exploration of antiestablishment, spiritually based, alternative lifestyles. Many such people had been raised by parents who had largely abandoned their own religious traditions in the aftermath of the Holocaust, driven by a desire to assimilate and a waning of belief. Coming of age at a time of great social ferment, in an environment that encouraged the celebration of multiculturalism and ethnic pride, these young people often became attracted to observant Judaism as a way to explore their ethnic heritage and Jewish identities. While a great many of these "returnees" adopted fully Orthodox lifestyles only temporarily, ultimately leaving Orthodox Judaism for other denominations, a good number of them remained. Malkie's parents were among the latter.

Having absorbed her parents' enthusiasm for and commitment to the Lubavitch way of life, when she was growing up, Malkie dreamed of becoming a good Hasidic wife, mother, and outreach worker, bringing Lubavitch's brand of Judaism to Jews across the globe. She loved the rebbe, and, like many others in her community, believed he was *Moshiach* (the Messiah). Excelling at school, Malkie was the valedictorian of her high-school class, and upon her graduation, she went off to seminary in Israel to hone her outreach skills. With that extra year of study under her belt, she would be ready for marriage, children, and a life of emissary work. As it turned out, however, things didn't go exactly according to plan.

In Israel, away from the insularity and security of Crown Heights, Malkie began to have serious questions and doubts. Did God really give the Torah to Moses at Sinai, or could human beings actually have written it? And who was the rebbe—the man whose picture adorned almost every Jewish home and store in Crown

Heights—and what was his place in all of this, anyway? There was no doubt that he was a great man, but was he really the Messiah, as she and so many others fervently believed, even after his death in 1994? Or was he just a regular human being, like everyone else?

While Malkie's questions were the product of her own keen intelligence and curiosity, their development was no doubt influenced by what was transpiring in Lubavitch at the time she was coming of age. In the 1980s, when Malkie was just a child, the Lubavitcher rebbe had begun talking about the coming of the Messiah. Many Lubavitchers eventually became convinced that the rebbe himself was the Messiah, and that the day he would reveal himself as such (known as the redemption day) was close at hand. Throughout the 1990s, this belief intensified within the Lubavitch community, and many felt that it was only a matter of days, or even hours, before the arrival of the redemption day. Some even believed that merely talking about the Messiah and the rebbe would expedite his revelation.

While the rebbe never explicitly claimed to be the Messiah, his enigmatic, mystical way of speaking nonetheless made it possible for many people to accept that interpretation. Cheering on huge crowds to sing "We want Moshiach now," the rebbe also did nothing to actively discourage the growing speculation that he was indeed the Messiah. In fact, when the rebbe became ill in the early 1990s, many of his Hasidim began to chant, "Long live our master, teacher, and rebbe king Messiah forever and ever," convinced that his illness was merely a test of their faith and prerevelation endurance.

After the rebbe's death in 1994, following a prolonged illness, fear and confusion overtook the Lubavitch community worldwide. Some believed that the rebbe wasn't really dead, because he was the Messiah, and the Messiah lives forever. Others accepted his death, believing that, while he was certainly worthy and capable of being the Messiah, the current generation had failed to do enough to bring about the realization of his revelation and the people's redemption.

The tension that emerged within the community over this issue created fertile soil for the growth of doubt and disillusionment.

As Malkie began to wonder during her year in Israel, if the rebbe wasn't actually Moshiach, but merely a normal human being, why should she have to live her life according to his dictates, submitting to all the rules and regulations of the community over which he presided, even in death? If the rebbe wasn't really connected in a direct line to God, did it make sense for thousands of people to make decisions about their lives based on what he said? Why should she, for example, have to accept the rebbe's view that she shouldn't go to college? While Malkie had always trusted his judgment about the perils of getting a secular education—after all, he had earned a technical degree in engineering from the Sorbonne and *still* believed his Hasidim should not attend college—her perspective was beginning to change. Maybe it was time to judge for herself.

As confused and deeply troubled as she was that year, Malkie kept these questions to herself, for the most part. On the rare occasions when she did voice them in class, she found her teachers' responses woefully insufficient. She knew that hers were the kinds of questions she might have to face in the course of her own outreach work, and it was quickly becoming apparent to Malkie that there was nobody who could provide her with satisfying answers. In fact, these questions only led to more—about the ultimate truth of the religion, the structure of the community, and the role of the rebbe. The way of thinking she had learned in the community wasn't holding up very well under her increasing scrutiny. In fact, it had become like a house of cards.

Before the year was out, Malkie had decided that she wanted to go to college, to read literature and philosophy, to learn about and experience the wider world so that she could come to her own conclusions. These desires were accompanied by a growing sense of unease about the arranged marriage she would be expected to enter into upon her return to Brooklyn. Of course, she wouldn't be forced to marry anyone against her will (Jewish law explicitly prohibits that), and she would have the option to wait a little, if she felt she needed more time. The problem was that Malkie felt she might need a lot more time—time to explore and act on her burgeoning curiosity about the world and her place in it. However, she knew that, were she to follow this path, she would no longer be able to live in her once beloved community. Nobody there would accept her decision. In fact, to most people in Crown Heights, it would come as a complete shock and a profound shame.

Malkie had no idea how she might break this news to her parents, although, during her time in Israel, they had become aware that something was up. How could she tell them—these people who had always shown her so much love, and whom she in turn had made so proud—that the life they had chosen to reject so many years ago was one she now desperately wanted to explore? Perhaps they would identify with her, given how radically they had broken with their own pasts. But Malkie's parents had chosen to become religious because, having already experienced the secular world, they believed that in Lubavitch they had found the truth. Being able to raise their nine children in such a community had been a blessing. They would never understand why Malkie no longer shared their feelings, and were instead likely to search for clues about where they had gone wrong, or what was wrong with their daughter.

And then there was the guilt, and the fear. How would Malkie explain all of this to her younger siblings? What would she say to the girls in the community who had admired and looked up to her for her knowledge and devotion, and whom she herself had counseled during their own times of confusion and doubt? Aside from all of this, Malkie also knew that leaving the community would be fraught with risk. Were she to pursue these new desires, she might well discover that the community had been right all along. The secular world might be a terrible place, filled with people lacking the right values and any sort of compassion. Without God's Torah and the community to guide her, maybe she would be lured into a life of drugs and sex and even crime. And by that time, it would be too late. She would be completely ruined—even though, given their eternal confidence in the essential truth of their worldview, the Lubavitchers would always welcome back to the fold someone who had gone off the path. Indeed, such people only helped to prove their point.

Finally, after months of emotional struggle in Israel and still more upon her return, Malkie summoned the huge amount of courage it took to pick up the phone one Shabbos, while her family was at shul, and reach out to a nonreligious cousin for help. Using the phone on Shabbos was, of course, a violation of Jewish law, but instead of the guilt she expected to feel, Malkie was overcome by a shocking sense of relief at the knowledge that, finally, her struggle had extended outside of herself. She would no longer have to deal with her feelings solely on her own. When her cousin answered the phone, Malkie could hardly speak. They agreed to meet at their grandmother's house the next day. Her heart was racing.

Malkie's decision to place that call ultimately led her to move out of her parents' home and in with her grandmother—across the river, but worlds away—in Manhattan. Throughout her childhood, Malkie's family had made weekly trips to see her grandparents, but Malkie had never really felt close to them—after all, they were assimilated. Her grandparents, though proud Jews, didn't keep kosher, didn't observe the Sabbath or observe any of the other mitzvot. They even had a TV, which was great, because the kids got to watch *Sesame Street* and *Barney*, if only for a little while. That suited everyone fine as, with the television on, there was little opportunity to discuss controversial topics, or anything else that might contradict the way the children were being raised. The family even brought their own food with them, and ate it with their own utensils.

Now, after all those years of regular but impersonal visits, Malkie found herself living in her grandmother's home, sleeping on her couch, and sharing her meals. As important as the food and the shelter, however, was having her grandmother's sympathetic ear and heart as she tried to make the transition to the secular world—a process that was filled with equal parts fear, excitement, and profound confusion.

Coming from a life in which God's laws literally governed which shoe to put on and tie first, Malkie quickly came to realize that the outside world had a completely different set of rules, and that their logic was often difficult to penetrate. When you ate out at a restaurant, for example, did you clean your own table when you were finished eating? If a boy spoke to you, did it mean he wanted to have sex, or that he assumed that you did? Why was it that everyone in her grandmother's apartment house had copies of the *New York Times* outside their front doors in the morning? Were secular people just as conformist in their apparent devotion to that newspaper, and whatever was in it, as the people from her community were with respect to carrying out God's laws and the teachings of the rebbe?

Within several months of moving in with her grandmother, Malkie applied and was accepted to Hunter College, the school her grandmother had attended over half a century before. Even though Malkie, unlike her male counterparts from Crown Heights, had a legitimate high-school diploma (the girls' school is certified by the New York Board of Regents), those first months of college were nonetheless extremely difficult. Not only was much of the subject matter new, but—at least as important—so also were the social conventions.

Malkie had never shared a classroom with boys, and she had no idea how she was supposed to act with them. When a professor told her to come by her office for a copy of the syllabus, she didn't know what that was, but she was too embarrassed to ask. When a fellow student referred to some popular TV show or film, she would be at a total loss. Growing up in a community where there was so much opportunity for effortless socializing, it was also difficult for Malkie to figure out how to make plans with people in advance, leaving her at times feeling particularly lonely and adrift. And, away from the community and its familiar rituals surrounding food preparation and meals, Malkie would often forgo eating altogether; choosing something to eat and eating it alone sometimes seemed harder than not eating at all. Much of the time, Malkie felt even more foreign than some of her classmates who had only recently emigrated from Russia or Senegal. In fact, she felt like an alien from another planet. And she feared others probably saw her this way as well.

Gradually, however, Malkie became a little more comfortable. She observed everything closely, like an anthropologist during her first weeks in the field, and slowly she began to adjust. She went to her first movie and eventually, with great angst, bought and wore her first pair of pants. She decided to enroll in a Biblical studies course at Hunter in order to see how "they"—people in the secular world —saw things. Through the class she became aware of possible interpretations of the Old Testament that differed from the ones she'd been taught. After some time, she even went to a few rock concerts, which were exciting and fun—although the worshipful crowds made her a bit uncomfortable, reminding her of the Lubavitch rallies of her childhood, at which literally thousands of black-clad Hasidic men would chant, hanging on the rebbe's every word. Throughout it all, her grandmother—along with several other non-religious relatives—was there, unwavering in her support. She could not resist, however, making occasional merciless fun of Malkie's understandable ignorance about so many of the ways of the outside world.

About three months after Malkie moved in with her, her grandmother was diagnosed with ovarian cancer. Now it was Malkie's turn to care for the woman who had been caring so well for her throughout this extremely complicated time. Juggling school and a full-time job, Malkie also did whatever she could to help her grandmother. When she was accepted to an exchange program at the University of Massachusetts in Amherst, she made sure she was home as many weekends as possible, to be at her grandmother's side.

Around this time, Malkie received a phone call from a young woman from another Hasidic community who had heard Malkie's story and was desperate to find a way out herself. Her situation sounded extremely difficult, and she seemed to be in great emotional distress. Malkie listened to her, even offered to meet, but knew that there was very little she could do to help. After all, unlike Malkie, this woman didn't have a sympathetic grandmother who was willing to take her in.

After days of being haunted by the young woman's call, Malkie decided that there was in fact something she could do, and she ran the idea by her ailing grandmother. She would create an organization in her grandmother's honor—a different kind of Chabad House, really. It would serve people who, like herself, felt a deep need to explore the world beyond the Hasidic community, but who had no place to turn to help them do it. She had discovered that an organization like this existed in Israel, where there is a lot more awareness among the general population about ultra-Orthodox or *haredi* life, and where tensions between secular Jewish Israelis and the *haredim* tend to make those in the secular society particularly sympathetic to people seeking to explore the world beyond haredi borders.

But this was not the case in America, where the vast majority of people outside the Hasidic world—even including other Jews—had little knowledge of its ways. To most of those Americans who even knew these communities existed, the Hasidim were a kind of curiosity, an intriguing remnant of the old world, mysteriously transported onto the streets of modern cities and, occasionally, even rural towns. Malkie knew that executing her plan would be a very difficult undertaking.

However, if her upbringing in Lubavitch had taught her anything, it had taught her that if she put all of her heart and soul into a goal, she could build something very big from almost nothing at all. And while Lubavitch (and the other Hasidic sects from which her organization would soon draw clients) would certainly disapprove of what she was setting out to do, it was at least in part the lessons she had learned in that community—to reach out and open one's heart and home to other Jews—that had given her the confidence to try. If people from her community would inevitably denounce her as troubled, misguided, possibly even anti-Semitic, Malkie's impulse to reach out to others in her position was, in fact, profoundly Jewish.

Malkie wasn't going to try to influence anyone to abandon the

Hasidic community, or the Jewish religion, for that matter. And she wasn't going to go into Hasidic neighborhoods and advertise or recruit. But, for people who might otherwise be at risk for all kinds of serious problems, she was going to offer a safe and supportive environment in which to ask questions, explore their options, and make their own decisions. She would provide counseling and job resources, tutoring in English and other necessary subjects, and access to social and cultural events and outings aimed at familiarizing people with secular society. Maybe someday she would even be able to offer temporary housing to those who had been cast out by their families and had nowhere else to go. In the most basic sense, to Malkie, this wasn't about rejecting religion or bashing her community, but about saving lives. And, as the Jewish tradition holds, in saving just one life, you save the entire world.

By the time I first met Malkie that day at Starbucks, she had begun to put her plans into action. She had created a board, and they had applied for nonprofit status. She had also enlisted the help of a social worker to run regular support groups for the people who had begun to contact her after learning—all by word of mouth—about what she was doing. In fact, after only the first few support group meetings, which were attended in almost equal numbers by people from Satmar and Lubavitch (along with a sprinkling of those who had grown up in other Hasidic groups), Malkie and the other participants began to joke that this was the only place on earth where members of the two sects actually managed to be together without a brawl erupting.[5]

Some people contacted Malkie because they were desperate for more personal or intellectual freedom than their community and family would tolerate. They were tired of feeling constrained, of concealing their desires and sneaking around. Many were single, but some were married, most often with children, and often their spouses didn't share their views. While some people wanted to continue being religious, others no longer did, or had already given up being observant—often in secret. Religion was particularly confusing for many, because in the Hasidic world, it was a black or white issue. Officially, one was either religious or not, and if anyone stopped observing the Sabbath or keeping kosher, it was as if he or she were no longer a Jew.

Malkie also began hearing from those who had already made the break, but were eager to share their experiences with others like themselves, and to get some help moving forward. And then there were the extremely disturbing stories of physical and sexual abuse, which began to surface over time, as people became more comfortable talking about their lives. It was hard for Malkie to know whether these experiences were more common among those who had left these communities—possibly a reason for their decision to break away—than in the general Hasidic population (or, for that matter, the general population beyond the Hasidic world), but the more she heard, particularly from the men, the more worrisome the subject became. Thank God she had never been subjected to anything like that.

Indeed, hearing the stories of others made Malkie all the more aware of how fortunate she herself had been. Although her grandmother had passed away many months before these calls became a regular feature of her daily life, hardly a week went by—as Malkie spoke and met with people from communities throughout New York, and sometimes far beyond—that she didn't feel grateful to her, and think about how impossible this transition would have been without the emotional support and practical guidance she had provided.

How, for example, would she have coped, had she been in a situation like Motti's? Through Malkie, I met Motti, a man in his late thirties who had grown up in Satmar, totally unaware of the outside world until he managed to get hold of a tiny radio, which he hid in his sock and listened to in school, through an earpiece concealed by his peyos. Like many of his classmates at the time, Motti was often disciplined physically by his teachers and neglected by his overwhelmed parents. As a little boy, he had been very attached to his mother, but as he grew older, the enforced separation of the sexes, as well the prohibition against any physical expression of affection between members of the opposite sex, made him feel all the more isolated and alone—a situation that he believes made him particularly easy prey for some of the older men in the community. On many occasions, these men would grope and fondle him in the men's mikvah, where Hasidic men are supposed to go to purify themselves before the Sabbath.

Of course, Motti never told anyone then about what had happened in the mikvah. At that time, childhood sexual abuse was hardly discussed even in the secular world, and in the Hasidic community—where talking openly about sex was and remains taboo—for Motti to even hint at such behavior could have gotten him into big trouble.

Indeed, while it is unclear whether or not such abuse exists to a greater degree in these communities than it does in the general population,[6] some have theorized that Jewish communities' historical antipathy toward informers[7] has likely played some role in keeping such abuse quiet, when it occurs.[8] The Yiddish word *moser* is used to describe those who betray the community to outside authorities (historically, the authorities of tsarist Russia or medieval Europe). *Messira*, or the act of informing, was once punishable by death, and remains a serious sin to this day.

While not explicitly articulated, this concept loomed large throughout Motti's childhood, communicated to him implicitly by his parents and the community. And so he kept these experiences to himself, suffering in silence. Indeed, the only time Motti ever really felt happy was when he tuned in to the outside world on his tiny radio. Listening to it, he would lose himself in a Yankees game, or in snippets of classical music, or in the ads that introduced him to often startling new information, such as the fact that car companies came out with new and improved models every year.

At seventeen, Motti decided to tell his parents that he wanted the opportunity to explore life outside the community—but that did not sit well with them, and soon he was spending his days on the streets and his nights on the subway, riding the longest routes possible so that he wouldn't have to wake up too many times to change trains. His English was terrible, and he knew no one outside of the Brooklyn Hasidic community where he had grown up. He did eventually find his way to a modern Orthodox yeshiva that was willing to take him in for a time, but he knew he wouldn't be able to stay there forever. Gradually, he began to make some contacts, and eventually he got work, at a succession of low-skill jobs. His parents wouldn't even take his phone calls. The years that followed were marked by problems with drugs and alcohol, financial pressures, and, at times, debilitating depressions.

By the time Motti got in touch with Malkie, his life was on a much better path. He had finally been able to save enough money for therapy, and had recently decided that he was ready to think about college. He had heard that Malkie had gone to college, and he wanted her help to do the same. He had no idea how to go about applying to college, or whether he could even afford to go. He didn't know what would be expected of him there, and wasn't sure he'd be able to handle it. But it was very important to him to try.

So, Malkie had agreed to do whatever she could for Motti, and was keeping up her end of the bargain by meeting with him regularly to work on his college essay and gather and complete the necessary paperwork for his application. She had confidence in him, she told me, when we first met. And, over time, Motti would prove himself worthy of that confidence by enrolling in his first semester of college almost exactly a year later.

But Malkie had met so many others who needed much more help than Motti—not just people who were still living in Hasidic communities and struggling to find a way out, but also those who had already taken that step. Many had complicated problems, problems that went beyond the basic needs of shelter and food, extending to every area of social life. It was almost as if such people had to learn everything again from scratch. For example, there was the young woman whose powerful desire to "make up for lost time"—coupled with her naïveté about the complicated rituals of dating—kept propelling her to invite men she had just met back to her apartment, often with disastrous consequences. She was also wondering whether in fact she was a lesbian, because, growing up, she had always had such intense relationships with other girls. The extreme sex segregation of the Hasidic world tends to mean that people's most intimate relationships occur with members of the same sex.

Then there was the man who had questioned everything from the time he was a little child. He had become so used to keeping his thoughts to himself that he now had tremendous difficulty trusting, let alone socializing with, other people. Even though he had managed to attend a community college, and to find a telemarketing job, his tendency to stay away from other people was as strong as ever. When he first met Malkie, he was smoking pot several times a day, just to make his inevitable social interactions bearable.

In fact, as Malkie explained to me, people in the community like to use these kinds of stories as warnings to others who might stray, as evidence of the evil that awaits anyone who falls off the path. It is true that a lack of preparation for life in the outside world has often caused people to experience terrible troubles. Many even believed that on some level they were getting what they deserved. However, it is hard to make that kind of argument about people who haven't actually acted on any of their feelings. Take, for example, the nineteen-year-old boy from the Ger sect who was still living at home with his extremely religious parents and siblings. He was so consumed by a terrifying hopelessness about choosing a different kind of life that he could rarely get out of bed before three o'clock in the afternoon, though his only crimes, so far, were his thoughts and his dreams.

At times, Malkie told me as we finished our coffee, she found all of these stories overwhelming, especially because these were issues she herself was still facing in her own life. But each time a new person contacted her, and she heard what he or she was going through, it gave her a renewed sense of purpose. For example, only a few days before she had received a call from a young man named Yossi. He had called late at night, from a pay phone somewhere way downtown. It sounded as if he had been crying. Malkie had agreed to meet him the next day at a Starbucks right off Union Square—ironically, only a few hundred feet from the park where small groups of young Lubavitch outreach workers often set up shop, trying to identify Jewish passersby and convince them to put on tefillin and light Shabbos candles.[9] Maybe I would want to meet him as well, Malkie suggested. He had a lot to say about what it was like for him to grow up Hasidic. And he knew his community inside out. He might even be able to help me with some translation work.

Chapter Seven

Becoming a Rock Star

Even though I have tried my best to dress modestly, not surprisingly it seems that everyone on the street can tell I am not from this largely Satmar community. From the stares we are getting as we navigate past all the women pushing strollers on Lee Avenue in Williamsburg, it is pretty clear that no one knows quite what to make of this pairing: me, in my straight, black, knee-length skirt and black boots, way too old to be an unmarried teenager (the only possible explanation in this community for having uncovered hair), and Yossi, six foot two, in full Hasidic regalia, his dark, scraggly beard grazing the collar of his stained white shirt. Together, we are on a mission to find a rare book that Yossi is convinced will help me with my research. He thinks they might have a copy of it at the *seforim* store down the street.

I have known Yossi for several months now—I got his number from Malkie Schwartz—and he has quickly become an invaluable resource, providing me with all kinds of information about the various Hasidic communities of Brooklyn and beyond. His extensive knowledge of Hasidic history, and specifically of the personalities that have shaped it both in Europe and America, has even enabled him to make a little money dealing in antique Judaica—a good thing, since he recently lost his job tutoring a teenage boy, the child of newly religious parents.

Apparently, one morning several weeks ago, Yossi arrived late to their tutoring session at a small shul in the boy's neighborhood. He got there just in time, however, to discover that his student, a practiced pyromaniac, had become restless waiting for him and had decided to set a fire in the room they were using to learn Talmud. The rabbi smelled the smoke, someone found a fire extinguisher, and, thankfully, in the end nobody was hurt. But now, with the boy installed indefinitely in a psychiatric ward, and Yossi taking considerable heat from the rabbi and the family for arriving late and leaving him unsupervised, he was out of a job. Yossi felt a little bit guilty about what had happened, but not too guilty. After all, how could anyone expect someone like him, with his own meshugas—staying out till all hours, drinking Joeys at the bar in order to forget about his troubles with his father and his life—to be responsible for a pyromaniac? He thought it was more or less like the blind leading the blind.

When we arrive at the seforim store, Yossi tugs nervously at his beard and instructs me to wait outside. He is going in first to check if it's OK for me to come into the store. Apparently, this is not the kind of place that is accustomed to female customers. Its shelves are lined mostly with religious books in Hebrew, which Hasidic women generally don't read (unlike the men, they aren't instructed in Biblical Hebrew beyond what they have to know for their prayers), and volumes in Hebrew and Yiddish on Hasidic history and lineage. It seems that my presence might somehow be disruptive to the men inside. After about a minute, Yossi reemerges and tells me that I can come in. The owner has assured him that they don't bite.

The crowded space is dark and quiet, set up like library stacks. Several heavily bearded men with long peyos, their tzitzit peeking out below their jackets, are poring over open books. It all feels very mysterious and forbidding to me, especially because nobody so much as glances in my direction. I can't help but be reminded of the Purim I spent in the home of a Hasidic family, where all the men gathered and ate and drank generous amounts of alcohol (Purim is a drinking holiday) in the wood-paneled, book-lined dining room, while the women remained in the hot kitchen, with the babies and the food, receiving costumed revelers and exchanging information about diapers, carriages, and places to get good deals on china.

To my own surprise, spending time among those women seemed much more appealing to me that afternoon than being in the dining room with all the men—or even going near it. After all, the women's talk of the universal, everyday concerns of home and family made it easy for me to relate to them. But, ultimately, I have no idea whether I might have been just as comfortable with the men; the closest I ever got to one was when I was instructed by my hostess to move up against the hallway wall so a male guest could make his drunken way to the bathroom without being forced into the immodest act of making eye contact with me.

After Yossi speaks to the owner of the store in Yiddish, the man disappears for a few seconds, returning with a slim, leather-bound volume. He says something to Yossi, who in turn informs me that the book costs eighteen dollars. When I try to hand the owner a twenty-dollar bill, he refuses to take the money, and I quickly realize I have committed a major faux pas. Hasidic codes of modesty prohibit this man from touching any woman who is not his wife, and, though he certainly could have taken the money without touching my hand, people often take extra precautions when even accidental contact could occur. This is known as "putting a fence around the law." It turns out that I should have put the money directly on the counter, as they make you do at the blackjack table when you're buying chips from the dealer.

Back out on the street, Yossi explains that, had we been alone in the store, the owner might not have made such a fuss about taking the money from me. He probably made a big show of things because there were other men around and he didn't want to look bad in front of them. But then again, Yossi concedes, this is Williamsburg, which tends to be a lot stricter about these things than his own community, in Boro Park. There, the men in business—even the very *frum* ones —aren't usually such sticklers, especially if they sense it could undermine a sale. In fact, Yossi has been planning to show me around Boro Park for some time now. With characteristic impulsivity, he suggests that we go today.

On the F train headed to Boro Park, among the typical New York array of ethnicities and nationalities, there are several men dressed like Yossi. There are also more than a few women wearing long suits and wigs and hats, with shopping bags from places like Macy's and H&M dangling from the handles of their well-appointed strollers. Sitting next to each other, with Yossi translating passages of the book out loud for me, we are receiving the same kinds of perplexed and slightly disdainful stares we got on the streets of Williamsburg. I point this out to Yossi, and, pausing to glance around the subway car, he finally says, "Eh, let them look."

Once off the subway, we walk toward Thirteenth Avenue, the main shopping street of the community. On our way, Yossi takes me to see Anshe Sfard, the shul where the famed tenor Yossele Rosenblatt, who was born to a Hasidic family in the Ukraine in 1882 and came to America in 1911, was the cantor for a few years in the late 1920s. Although Rosenblatt remained Orthodox throughout his life, he nonetheless became a big star of the music world of his day, performing across the country (although he ultimately turned down an offer to perform opera) and attracting fans among Jews and non-Jews alike. In fact, Yossi tells me that in 1927 Rosenblatt was offered $100,000 by Warner Brothers to play Al Jolson's father in *The Jazz Singer*. He refused the role, however, because it would have required him to sing *Kol nidrei*—the opening words for the cancellation of vows, recited on the eve of Yom Kippur—in a stage setting. Ultimately, the producers were able to convince him to appear in a scene of the film as himself, singing nonliturgical music in a concert setting. Yossi would like to take me inside the shul, but because there are no women around, and I am not allowed in the men's section with him, we decide not to go in.

We then continue on toward the Bobov shul and yeshiva, where men from the largest Hasidic sect in Boro Park daven and learn. As we approach the building, with its twelve windows depicting the Hebrew months, the first thing that comes to Yossi's mind to tell me about is a Hasidic *alter kakher* he knew as a kid. The old man was so frail he could hardly walk himself to shul, but when he began to pray, his body would "fill with such a spirit" that he would straighten up to "ten feet tall, shaking with a fire for God." The second thing that comes to Yossi's mind is the story that circulated in the community several months ago about a very pious Bobover man who had invested a substantial portion of his savings in a fund managed by someone at the yeshiva. Upon learning that the entire fund had been lost, the man exacted his revenge by defecating in front of the shul's main office. Along with the only donation he could apparently still afford to make, the man also left a note in Yiddish that read, roughly: "Bobov has been shitting on me all my life; now I am shitting on Bobov." Needless to say, there was much speculation about what exactly had transpired and why, and every day for several weeks, jokes circulated in shul and in the men's mikvah about the incident: Was this a real Jewish terror attack, done on the cheap, without spending any money on weaponry? Clearly, this guy had given a donation from the bottom of his heart!

Yossi decides he wants to show me one of his favorite local haunts, a used book store. When a religious person wants to get rid of sacred books, it is customary to pay to have them buried, like a person. When Yossi was a teenager, he worked collecting books for burial, and often kept the best ones for himself. This store is owned by an open-minded Hasid in his fifties, who knows Yossi and often calls him up when something of particular interest finds its way to his store. The place is packed so tight with books—secular and religious works in Yiddish and Hebrew and other languages as well—that it is almost impossible to move without causing an avalanche. The owner isn't around, but a few minutes after we arrive, a man in a black suit and hat, with long peyos and tzitzit, emerges from the back and sidles up to Yossi. In hushed tones, he inquires about some old letters Yossi once told him about, written from the Bobover rebbe to the man's grandfather. He would like to buy them and wants to know what Yossi's contact is asking. The man scribbles something on a piece of paper, hands it to Yossi, and then quickly disappears down a flight of stairs into the basement.

In the area just to the left of the front door, we notice three large cardboard boxes bulging with books. Further investigation reveals that they were dropped off only about an hour earlier, by a mysterious, hunchbacked, dark-skinned old man wearing a white caftan and a long gray beard. Before I know it, Yossi is combing through the books, searching for signs of value—a signature, or the mark of a first edition. Some of the books are compelling enough for him to open and skim. After about twenty minutes, my eyes itching from the dust, I am compelled to pry him out of the place.

Near the bookstore we pass a *shatnes* "lab"—a place that determines whether garments contain the halachically prohibited mixture of linen and wool. According to Yossi, people routinely bring their clothes to a shatnes tester because, while labels will usually tell what a suit or dress is made of, they often don't contain information about the material used in the collars or seams. A shatnes tester is trained to determine the precise makeup of the fabric, and he is also skilled at separating the linen from the wool, or the wool from the linen, so that, if he does discover that such a mixture is present, he can repair the garment, and its owner can wear it without violating Jewish law. Nobody knows exactly why this prohibition exists. Yossi explains to me that the Torah is divided into three categories: *Mishpatim* (Laws), *Eidus* (Testament to God), and *Chukim* (Statutes). Authoritative opinion on the Talmud holds that Mishpatim are rational laws—that is, laws that would have been created by people on their own, even if God had not commanded them, such as laws against stealing or killing. Chukim are laws that cannot be understood within a rational context, and are observed only because God has commanded their observance. Shatnes is understood to be a *Chok*, and to strictly religious Jews, it is no less binding than the dietary laws.

As we walk, Yossi points out the many houses in the throes of expansion, covered in scaffolding, boasting signs for contractors and construction companies. Large Hasidic families can often benefit from more square footage than many of these dwellings originally possessed, and some people have found architecturally creative ways to add rooms to their typically overcrowded homes. Yossi claims that some people who run out of money before the additions are completed have developed creative solutions to that problem as well—like the man who dealt with his inability to pay his mortgage by changing his name, putting his house in the new name, and then obtaining a death certificate for his old self. He was reborn a few days later with a new Social Security number, but without his old financial troubles. Some people who are pressed financially will legally designate their basements or other parts of their houses as *shtieblech*, or small synagogues, and receive tax breaks because their homes are houses of worship. Someone who temporarily moves in with a friend whose home is designated a *shtiebl* can claim that he himself is homeless and sleeping in a synagogue, thus becoming eligible for Section 8 housing vouchers from the government.

In fact, in the late 1990s, the Hasidic village of New Square, in upstate New York, came under investigation for a plot by village leaders to underreport their income and boost their Section 8 rent subsidies. The scheme also involved funneling government money through a fictitious yeshiva that existed only as an address. According to published reports of the case,[1] the defendants paid village residents to "enroll" in the "yeshiva" so that they could apply for Pell grants from the government, which were then used to pay the defendants' salaries as "mentors" and "administrators" in the nonexistent school, and to purchase the building. The four men were also convicted of setting up a shell corporation in order to receive $100,000 in small business loans, money that was instead distributed to a variety of community concerns. The investigation resulted in the convictions of four village leaders, whose sentences were later commuted by Bill Clinton around the time of his wife's bid for the U.S. Senate seat from New York.

When I tell Yossi that I find all of this fairly appalling, he assures me that I can go into any shul or men's mikvah, where guys are always sharing the latest tactics and strategies, and hear even more for myself (which of course, being a woman, I can't). After all, these are men who study law all day and learn how to think critically and spot loopholes. In fact, Yossi tells me that when he recently saw a commercial on TV with a guy running up and down the steps of the Capitol in Washington, shouting about all of the unclaimed millions in available government grants, and advertising his book enumerating them, he knew the man had nothing on the Hasidim, who probably could have written an even better book. Of course, a lot of these schemes are ethically dubious at best, he agrees with me, but many of the people around here came from places in Eastern Europe and Russia where they were forced to find ways to work the system, as legitimate channels of making a living were often closed to them due to discrimination. Here in America, the situation is different, but apparently the mentality often remains the same. Perhaps, Yossi offers with a laugh, this is just another way of maintaining tradition.

We finally make our way onto Thirteenth Avenue, which is heavily trafficked and lined with a wide variety of stores: kosher butchers, bakeries, and fishmongers; men's and women's clothiers, wig shops, and cell phone dealers; pizza parlors, kosher takeout joints, and even the obligatory Korean deli. We also pass a relatively new-looking kosher hotel, as well as a Jewish music and video store and a modern, spacious, and well-stocked Judaica emporium, called Eichler's, boasting a large selection of books in English and Yiddish and Hebrew. While almost everyone on the street (save for a few Italians and newly arrived Eastern Europeans, who often work in the community as maids) is dressed according to Orthodox standards, the Jewish population here appears to be much more diverse and prosperous than it is in Williamsburg.

In Williamsburg, most of the women we saw on the street were wearing navy suits, opaque, flesh-colored stockings with seams up the back, and scarves on their heads. Here, there is more variation in women's styles of dress (more brightly colored suits, long skirts paired with stylish long-sleeved sweaters and funky denim skirts and even sneakers on some of the teenage girls), and most of them seem to be wearing well-coiffed, expensive shaitels, made from human hair. (In fact, many of these wigs will be burned publicly in the streets a few months from now, when several Israeli rabbis will issue a ban on wearing wigs made from Indian hair used in Hindu religious rituals. The rabbis will claim that these wigs were somehow implicated in "idol worship," which is prohibited by Jewish law. Some women will quietly resist this ruling, however, and ignore the posters and flyers urging them to buy synthetic wigs—why should they allow thousands of dollars to go up in smoke for something so inconsequential? Others will forgo the burning and instead donate their wigs to cancer patients. Yossi's mother, at his father's behest, will consider wearing an ugly synthetic wig, before ultimately settling on a *tichel*, or plain scarf, instead. And Yossi will conclude that the rabbis who made the ruling must all be investors in a synthetic wig company.)

As we walk along the avenue, Yossi passes a few young men he knows. While he manages to escape the notice of some of them by pretending to stare intently into the windows of stores, others see him and stop to greet him. Nervous about what these people might make of my presence, and whom they might tell about this chance encounter, Yossi skips the introductions, prompting me to try to look busy with my cell phone, or consumed by some faraway sight. Near Fifty-fifth Street, Yossi spots a close friend walking with his wife and two young children. If his friend were alone, Yossi tells me, he would run up to meet him. However, because the man's wife hasn't so much as given Yossi's phone messages to her husband ever since Yossi shaved (he wasn't even invited to attend their son's *bris*), he determines it's best to let them go. Yossi seems to feel completely at home on the streets of his neighborhood. It's just the neighbors that seem to be a problem.

Just then, Yossi abruptly takes a right turn off the avenue—on this block, he tells me, is a *sofer*, or ritual scribe, who makes his living copying Jewish sacred texts, by hand, for use in *mezuzahs* and tefillin, Torahs and *megillahs*. There are very strict regulations about the way the letters and words must be formed; while some mistakes may be corrected, others render the entire effort irredeemable, requiring the sofer to begin the process again, from scratch. There are also very exacting standards for the ink; its color and durability, as well as its composition, are regulated—only kosher products may become a part of it. Yossi explains to me that some sofers even purify themselves in the mikvah before they begin their work. Many believe that the spiritual thoughts the sofer has while writing can transmit extra spiritual clarity and strength to the reader.

Yossi locates the place, a basement apartment in the middle of the block. We ring the bell and are soon greeted by a short, heavyset man, dressed in Hasidic garb. He smiles warmly and welcomes us inside. Yossi speaks to the man in Yiddish, and the sofer then turns to me and asks, "So, you want to see what I do?" A little girl in a pink dress is running up and down the hall, giggling. The man leads us into his workroom, where several long tables and file cabinets are covered with books, bottles of ink, brushes, parchment, magnifying lamps, and other tools and instruments. The man shows us what he is working on: a Torah scroll. The meticulous, painstaking work on this scroll will take him close to a year to complete, for which he will be paid $20,000. It is beautiful.

As we are leaving the sofer's apartment, Yossi tells me that we are very close to his grandmother's house, where he is currently staying. He asks me whether I would like to meet her. By now, she and I have spoken several times on the phone, and it appears that she is fairly unconcerned about Yossi's involvement with me—unlike his father. Having listened in on one of Yossi's and my phone calls one day when Yossi was back home to pick up some of his belongings, Yossi's father got my number from his caller ID box. Luckily, I wasn't at home to receive his call, but he left me a message, warning me never to speak to his son again, assuring me that Yossi had no interest in my "void," secular life, and proclaiming his belief that all secular Jews were uncaring people who only wanted to turn a son against his parents.

Yossi's grandmother lives in a large, three-story house, which she and her late husband bought at just the right time. Now it is worth about three times what they paid for it, and, with little use for so much space, she rents the top two floors to a Hasidic family. When we arrive at the house, Yossi rings a bell and his grandmother buzzes us in. She is in her mid-seventies, dressed tastefully in a black skirt, black and white striped sweater, and short grayish-blonde wig that looks as if it could be her own hair. She immediately asks us whether we are hungry and ushers us into her large, sparkling kitchen, through a hallway whose walls boast several innocuous paintings of flowers (no graven images here).

She is not exactly demonstrative, and even seems a bit harried—what with helping her daughter and keeping the house in good order and going here and there to see all of the grandchildren, she has no time for anything. But over the next hour or so, she will reveal a sharp sense of humor, the savvy of someone who grew up on the vibrant, multiethnic streets of Brooklyn, and a concern for Yossi's well-being, manifest in her rapid-fire badgering of him about whether he has had enough to eat today, if he has heard from his father, or about any new job prospects, or if he's had his Medicaid card renewed, or needs anything washed. When he assures her everything is OK with him today, she brings in some photographs to show me of her husband and family, spanning the years from the 1950s until today. She points out how her husband's beard got longer and his clothes more Hasidic over time. She says she misses him.

After Yossi and I consume half a bag of potato chips and several glasses of ginger ale, I tell him I have to get going. I am supposed to meet somebody in another part of Brooklyn for dinner. He asks me whether he can come along, and then immediately tells me to forget it, that he didn't mean to be rude and doesn't want to intrude. I tell him that I don't think it will be a problem if he joins us. Stan is my aunt's boyfriend's brother. He grew up in Brownsville, not too far from Yossi's grandmother, speaking Yiddish at home with his parents. I am sure he will be thrilled to meet Yossi.

As we walk back to the subway stop, Yossi's cell phone starts to ring. His grandmother just got the phone for him a few days ago, and he is still a little unsure how it works. Finally, he manages to answer it. It's his father. Yossi has no idea how he got the number; Yossi certainly didn't give it to him. His father asks him where he is and if he has put on tefillin today, or learned (the Hasidic idiom for "studied"). Things would be much better for him if he would only put on tefillin. Yossi keeps repeating, "OK" into the phone and, after about a block, hangs up. He tells me that he is afraid his father will never understand him, that he won't even try. The whole situation makes him very angry. Then, suddenly, his brow lifts. He is very excited to meet this Stan, he says.

We arrive at Stan's apartment, and within minutes he and Yossi are speaking to each other exclusively in Yiddish. Before long, they are discussing the Yiddish theater and Molly Picon, one of the big stars of the Yiddish stage and screen. Stan tells Yossi he wants to take him to the Second Avenue Deli, where there is a whole room filled with Yiddish movie posters. Yossi says he can't wait.

As they are talking, I notice a small box full of clothes sitting over near Stan's bedroom door. It is filled with pairs of jeans, cotton shirts, and sweaters. I ask him what the clothes are there for, and he tells me he is giving them to charity, that they are a little worn, don't fit as well as they used to. Then, as if reading my mind, he suddenly offers them to Yossi. Yossi's a little bit taller than Stan, but they both have slim builds. Some of the things might actually fit.

Yossi is ecstatic. He walks right over to the box and removes a pair of jeans and a blue shirt. "Hey, what do you say?" he exclaims, holding up the clothes.

"Try them on," Stan says, directing Yossi toward the bathroom.

A few minutes later, Yossi emerges from the bathroom. The jeans actually fit, and the shirt works, too. Self-conscious about his peyos, which are growing back but still short, Yossi asks whether Stan has a bandanna; he has seen guys on the street wearing bandannas and likes the look. Within seconds, Stan produces a blue bandanna and helps Yossi fasten it around his head. Yossi finds his way to a full-length mirror, and he is transfixed. This is the first time since he was a small child that he has ever worn anything other than a black suit and white shirt. He removes his glasses and puts them back on again, leaning close to the mirror, inspecting every inch of himself. It is as if he is taking the measure of a total stranger.

"What do you think of the beard?" Yossi asks us nervously. "Can you still tell I am a Hasid?" With the blue bandanna and the long, wild beard and glasses, Yossi suddenly looks like a cross between Che Guevara and Osama bin Laden. It's a look that would certainly fly in the East Village, or among the artists and hipsters in non-Hasidic Williamsburg, or even here, over on Smith Street. Yossi asks us if we will go outside with him. He wants to see how people will react.

As the three of us walk up the block, a huge smile brightens Yossi's face. Maybe, he asks us, someone will mistake him for a rock star?

Chapter Eight

Second Acts

For over ten years, Yitzchak Fine was his Hasidic community's version of a rock star, packing a large lecture hall full of men night after night, earning the admiration and praise of hundreds. Even women in his community were aware of his reputation. While they were not allowed to attend his classes on Talmud (even if the subject matter hadn't been off-limits to them, the prohibition against mixed seating would still have barred them from being present), most heard about his brilliance from their fathers, husbands, brothers, or sons, all of whom flocked to hear him, hanging on his every word.

What none of these admirers knew, however, was that when Yitzchak was not giving his lectures, he was often somewhere forty miles south, on the Upper West Side of Manhattan—a neighborhood he refers to as his "Jerusalem"—usually wearing jeans and a colorful shirt or sweater, with his long peyos tied in a knot over his head and covered with a baseball cap. During those forays, Yitzchak took advantage of all the culture Manhattan has to offer, with non-Hasidic friends who couldn't care less that he considers himself a feminist who believes that women can wear pants.

The men who attended Yitzchak's lectures for all those years also had no idea that, despite keeping kosher and observing the Sabbath, Yitzchak doesn't actually believe in their idea of God.

The first time I hear about Yitzchak Fine I am in the library of the Jewish Theological Seminary, doing research with Yossi. Even though Yossi has begun changing into Stan's hand-me-downs on the train heading into Manhattan—a kind of Hasidic Superman using the subway like his own personal phone booth—on this particular day, he has accidentally left his "civilian" clothes at his grandmother's house and is instead dressed like a Hasid. About ten minutes after the two of us sit down, a clean-shaven young man wearing a knit yarmulke, sweatshirt, and jeans approaches our table. He is a rabbinical student at the seminary. He overheard Yossi making some less than glowing remarks to me about the situation of women in the Hasidic world, and he is curious to know what we are doing here together.

I am not exactly sure how to respond—getting to know Yossi has made me particularly sensitive to those "enforcer" types he has encountered so many times before, the strangers who see fit to scold him for eating in nonkosher restaurants, or using the computer at the public library on Saturday. Even though he always makes sure in such situations to remove his kippah, apparently the black suit, white shirt, and scraggly beard still give him away to those with a discerning eye, who understand the significance of the limited color palette. Now, I am wondering whether *I* am about to be reprimanded for talking to a Hasidic man, or sitting too close to him. As if reading my mind, or likely just reacting to what's going through his, Yossi gets up from the table without a word. He quickly disappears into the stacks.

It turns out that we had no cause for concern. The young man tells me that if I want to learn more about gender in the Hasidic community, he knows of a wonderful Hasidic man who is particularly interested in women's issues. He would probably be happy to talk to me. His name is Yitzchak Fine and, though he is a devout Hasid, he also lectures students at various modern Orthodox yeshivas, which is in fact where the two of them met some time ago. Yitzchak is very open, he tells me, and a complete and utter genius. The rabbinical student gives me Yitzchak's e-mail address, and when he is at a safe distance from me, Yossi reappears. The student is right, he tells me. Yitzchak Fine is a very big deal.

So, I decide I will e-mail Yitzchak Fine. Not surprisingly, in his reply, he suggests we meet at Starbucks.

Yitzchak arrives at our meeting precisely on time, wearing the familiar ensemble: white shirt, black pants, black velvet kippah. In his late thirties, he is trim and energetic, with lively blue eyes and a long, dark, bushy beard. His peyos are detectable only upon close inspection, rolled up and held into place behind his ears, as I will later learn, with hair gel. His English, though slightly accented, is excellent.

Yitzchak asks me to tell him about my research, and, not knowing anything about him beyond what little the rabbinical student told me, I am not sure how he might react. I explain that I am trying to learn about the experiences of people who are struggling to live within the symbolic boundaries of the Hasidic world. I say that I am not sure how this might be relevant to him, but that the student who put us in touch had indicated that Yitzchak had an interest in women's issues.

Yitzchak listens attentively and tells me that he is indeed very interested in the lives of Hasidic women, particularly their inner lives. As a man, however, he isn't permitted the kind of contact with women that might help him gain any significant insight into this issue; even his ex-wife, to whom he had been married for many years, remained something of a mystery to him. He tells me that he has some relatively open-minded female relatives he could put me in touch with, if I would like. He is sure that, even as an outsider, I, being a woman, would probably be able to learn more from them than he could ever find out. After about fifteen minutes, Yitzchak excuses himself from the table—his parking meter is running out, and he has to be on his way—but assures me that he will talk to his relatives and get back to me as soon as he does.

Over the next few weeks, Yitzchak and I begin to exchange e-mail, and sometimes Instant Messages as well, when I notice his screen name pop up on my buddy list late at night. As promised, he sends me contact information for a sister-in-law and a female cousin, who both claim they would be happy to talk to me. And then, little by little, he begins to reveal more about himself, and his rather complicated relationship to his Hasidic community. The most intriguing and poignant of these revelations comes in an e-mail response to a question I send him about male-female relationships among the Hasidim:

> *Hey!*
>
> *What's most surprising to me is that most people in this community aren't aware how much they're missing out of life. You and I and most NORMAL people take the centrality and necessity of love, passion and intimacy for granted, around here people don't. If you ask them if they regret not ever having been in a loving relationship, most of them would say no.*
>
> *I remember, I was once listening to some cheesy, pop love songs and I asked my mom to listen too. She said to me "I've never been in such a situation, those sentiments don't appeal to me." Shocking, but also sad. I feel so sorry that they miss out of so much of what it means being human. Love, feelings and passion is what distinguishes us from all other creatures.*
>
> *I think there is some good old Darwinism involved. In order to survive, their bodies have evolved so that they don't have those needs; they adapted genetically, they don't have a physical need for any deep emotional attachments and experiences. Once you separate sex from feelings it's easy to see how some people become deviant. Sexual gratification becomes an animalistic pursuit, devoid of beauty and passion and meaning.*

It is striking to me how Yitzchak refers to the members of his community as "they," and it is probably no accident that he also enlists Darwin—hardly a hero to the strictly Orthodox, who are not supposed to believe in evolution—to make his case. It is also fascinating that the Hasidic community, which infuses everyday activities with great holiness, apparently treats the realm of human relationships in just the opposite way. Yitzchak seems to be suggesting that the community's professed efforts to preserve the sacredness of sexual relations through the use of strict laws governing physical contact and the expression of affection have, in practice, made it much easier for such relationships to be profaned. Apparently, the secular world does not have a monopoly on loveless sex.

The rabbinical student's description notwithstanding, it quickly becomes clear to me that Yitzchak does not consider himself a Hasid, or at least that he doesn't identify as a member of the larger Hasidic community. In fact, after we have been acquainted for many weeks, Yitzchak and I have quite a laugh when he discovers that the student who put us in touch did so precisely so that Yitzchak could dispel some of the negative opinions about Hasidic life that he had overheard Yossi expressing to me in the library. It seems that when he feels he needs to, Yitzchak is pretty good at keeping things to himself.

Over time, and as we get to know each other better, Yitzchak begins to unravel for me how he came to lead a double life for so long, and how he has finally managed to integrate his two worlds into one.

According to Yitzchak, there was no precise moment he can point to when he stopped believing in Hasidic theology, or in his community's way of life. It was more like a process—a process that began when he was sixteen, the year he went away to study in a yeshiva in Israel. It is not uncommon for Hasidic boys to go to Israel after high school and before they get engaged. Some who go are serious scholars who want to take advantage of the opportunities for study there, while others are sent because they have been having trouble or "acting out" in their home communities; perhaps they have tried drugs, or maybe even sex. Some adults seem to believe that a stint in the Holy Land will resolve these issues, or at least allow them to be forgotten. Israel, however, is not always the panacea many hope it will be, and often boys who arrive with problems find that those problems actually worsen while they are there.[1] Fortunately, however, Yitzchak was not one of those boys—experimenting with drugs and sex had never had any appeal for him—but being in Israel created other problems.

When Yitzchak first arrived in Israel, he "frummed out," or became a lot more religious than he had been at home. Little by little, however, he began to meet people, travel around, and read new things, like the daily papers, which he had never done in the United States. For the first time in his life, Yitzchak was also exposed to secular Jews who were actually learned in Jewish law and philosophy. In fact, many of these types wrote editorials in the newspapers he was reading, often using their own substantial knowledge of Judaism to argue against haredi practices and positions on public policy, but doing so on haredi terms, using haredi language. Yitzchak found this both startling and thrilling. He was pretty sure that people in America didn't debate Jewish law in the mainstream newspapers. When Jews made up the majority, Jewish issues were everybody's concern. And when Jews made up the majority, it seemed they were not afraid to fight with each other publicly—and, in Israel, fight they did.

It was eye-opening for Yitzchak to see that there were Jews who actually knew as much as he did about Jewish law—in some cases, having grown up in strictly religious families—but who had come to vastly different conclusions than the people in his community about how to live in the world. When such people argued, as they often did, that strictly Orthodox Jews were misreading the tradition, and when they could quote Jewish texts to support their arguments, Yitzchak realized that they couldn't be written off as merely ignorant. Unlike so many Reform and secular Jews in the United States, who often had very little Jewish education, these people knew what they were talking about.

And they also had tremendous knowledge of other, secular subjects as well, something that Yitzchak, to his growing dismay, surely lacked. In fact, he vividly recalls reading one article in which the writer demonstrated how a particular Jewish ritual practice had parallels in other religious traditions. Suddenly he realized that what he thought was unique to "beautiful Judaism" often derived from pagan rites that had influenced not only Jewish practice, but that of other religious traditions as well. Suddenly, it became very hard for Yitzchak to see the same degree of meaning in the rituals he had practiced all his life; in fact, it became hard to see in them any meaning at all. For, if the very things his community claimed to be revealed truth were really no more than social practices reflecting a particular historical context, then, far from being sacred, they could only be seen as really quite mundane. Yitzchak knew he needed to learn more.

At this point, Yitzchak still had no intention of abandoning the Hasidic way of life, despite his serious questions and growing curiosity about the world beyond what he had always known. He still loved and respected his parents immensely, and believed it was his obligation to them to follow their way of life, as they fully expected him to. So, upon his arrival back in the U.S., Yitzchak got engaged, the Hasidic way, after only two dates. He didn't know what he was getting into.

Within a few months of the wedding, Yitzchak realized that he and the girl he had married had turned out to be a terrible match. His wife was a good person, but she clearly was no more right for him than he was for her. They simply didn't want the same things out of life, and didn't share the same interests. If only they had been able to get to know each other just a little bit better. How could the matchmaker have made such a big mistake?

And then it struck him: if his parents and the community had been so wrong about this shidduch, was it possible that they could be wrong about other things as well? Maybe his faith in the wisdom of the community and its way of doing things had been grossly misplaced. Maybe they really had no idea about *anything*. Despite these concerns, however, Yitzchak worried about the personal and social ramifications of separating from his wife, the impact it would have on his family and on his and his wife's futures. At the time, divorce wasn't at all common in the community. He resigned himself to trying to find a way to live with the marriage, and when his wife became pregnant, any hopes he harbored of finding a way out were immediately extinguished.

Yitzchak dealt with his unhappiness by going out at night. Usually, he would drive down to Manhattan to see movies, go to museums, attend lectures, or hang out in bookstores, which he had begun to treat as his own personal libraries. He claims that he didn't start out doing any of this with the intention of rejecting his way of life, but, on the contrary, with the hope of finding answers that would make him more comfortable remaining in it. At first, he tried to set limits for himself: he would read only sociology, not theology or philosophy. But then he found that these fields were intertwined, and the web became bigger. Reading Kant led him to Hegel, and Hegel led to Marx. Marx took him to Nietzsche, and then Nietzsche to Freud. And somewhere along the line, Yitzchak made his way back to the Ba'al Shem Tov himself. The more he read, the more, he realized, he had to read. He couldn't stop. At a certain point, Yitzchak came to the conclusion that there was no way to make this Hasidic life work for him intellectually. But he had a family he needed to support, and so he decided to "put up that farce, put up that façade."

So, Yitzchak kept up wearing the garb, and prayed when he was supposed to. And even though he never violated the Sabbath or ate nonkosher food (he felt it was important to maintain some sense of integrity), in his mind he had left Hasidism behind. Not surprisingly, living like this was far from easy. In fact, there was a time when Yitzchak felt so trapped in his life that he actually became suicidal. Looking back, he is still not sure whether his sense of hopelessness had more to do with his difficult marriage or with the constraints of the Hasidic lifestyle—although, to his mind, the two were inextricably linked, the former a direct result of the latter.

His suffering, and his desire to explore the outside world on his own, certainly weren't easy on his wife, either. At one point, she became suspicious that he was going into the city to have sex with other women, which in fact he never did. He tried to explain to his wife that he wasn't interested in "having sex with a billion women," that he was going into the city because he *had* to, because he just couldn't bear feeling so suffocated in the community. Eventually, his wife came to believe him, and, for a time, that made the situation between them a little easier.

Indeed, Yitzchak always made a point of being honest with his wife, as well as his parents. And, together, they in turn kept his secrets from the rest of the community—in which, it turned out, he was steadily gaining a very big reputation as a formidable scholar, constantly in demand to lecture and teach. Yitzchak actually loved the intellectual stimulation of learning and teaching. However, he resented having to toe the party line in the classes he was paid to give. After all, there were so many other ways to look at the law, and so many exciting discussions and debates they could have about how it had developed and what it all meant.

But this would never fly in his community. To suggest this kind of inquiry in public would be the supreme act of self-sabotage. Just one sentence could cost Yitzchak his livelihood, and irrevocably damage the esteem in which so many in the community had come to hold him. How utterly meaningless his erudition would suddenly become to the men he taught—and to those who paid his salary—if they ever found out he was a nonbeliever. Even becoming modern Orthodox would have likely meant the end of his teaching career in the community. And Yitzchak knew he lacked the credentials that would enable him to find a decently paid, challenging job anywhere else.

Sometimes Yitzchak resented the fact that he couldn't tell his students what he really thought, who he really was. There were days when he felt furious that he was forced by his position to maintain the garb, beard, and peyos as indicators of his membership in a group to which he no longer believed he truly belonged. And sometimes he didn't care at all, laughing to himself at what he was pulling off.

The fact was, Yitzchak had actually come to have a great deal of affection for the men he taught, even if he regarded the overwhelming majority of their most deeply held beliefs as "primitive" and "backwards." How could you blame them, really? They hadn't been exposed to anything else. And, even despite the wildly distorted views many of them held about the outside world, these men were unfailingly warm toward Yitzchak. Indeed, he has always felt that one of the best things about his community is the genuine caring and support people give to and receive from each other, extended to anyone they regard as one of them. His explorations in the secular world have shown him that this is an exceedingly rare and precious thing.

Keeping his activities to himself, and continuing to move between his own community and his various haunts on the Upper West Side and beyond, Yitzchak slowly began to make some acquaintances, and even some friends, in the outside world. Some were people he had met during the long hours he spent reading in the library of the Jewish Theological Seminary. Others he had gotten to know through the growing number of lectures he attended at the seminary and other Jewish institutions in Manhattan. Eventually, one of these people told him about a job that he thought Yitzchak should apply for, a teaching position at a modern Orthodox girls' school in Queens. He would need to submit a resume before he could get an interview, but there was no doubt he was qualified for the job.

Yitzchak knew that, to the people in his community, teaching in a modern Orthodox school would be bad enough, and teaching girls even worse. Apparently, there is a prohibition in the Talmud against teaching religious subjects to women because they are "dull," and because they ask too many stupid questions. In Yitzchak's community, this prohibition is taken seriously, but Yitzchak still wanted to apply for the job—desperately. He thought his community's views about teaching women were ridiculous. Furthermore, this could be a chance for him to interact with more open-minded people. It might lead to other opportunities outside the community, as well. And with a growing family (three daughters by now), he could certainly use the money.

But his wife didn't see things this way. In fact, she didn't like the idea at all. They began to fight a lot and, as Yitzchak was offered and then accepted the job, he and his wife finally broached the subject of divorce. For Yitzchak, living together had become worse than whatever he could imagine would result from their divorce, and his wife felt the same. They decided to separate. But in order to get a religious divorce, which is required if one wants to remarry in the Orthodox community, they had to go to a rabbi. To Yitzchak's shock and horror, the rabbi refused to grant them the divorce, contending that the only reason Yitzchak wanted out of the marriage was that he had become modern, like a shaigetz.

So, for a time, Yitzchak would "frum out," pretend he was more religious, trying to build a better case for himself. But he could never keep it up for long. And then his wife abruptly changed her mind and wanted to try to make the marriage work. Yitzchak would have none of it, however, and after four years, the rabbi finally gave up and granted them their divorce.

Yitzchak believes that the experience of trying to end his marriage has something to do with his becoming what he considers an extreme feminist. Throughout the divorce proceedings, Yitzchak claims, the evidence the rabbi tried to use to prove that he was a heretic was the fact that he taught girls. It is precisely this way of thinking that makes Yitzchak so furious, particularly when he sees how it plays out in the community, and even in his own family. For example, when he was growing up, his mother would speak English to his sisters and Yiddish to his brothers, reflecting, he believes, the community's view that it doesn't matter if a woman is exposed a little to secular culture; it is the men who cannot risk being corrupted because, with their religious knowledge, they are simply more important to the community.

Of course, Yitzchak has heard countless times, and even taught, that the woman is the guardian of the Jewish home and family, responsible for the nurturing of future Jewish generations. And he knows all the arguments—better than most, in fact—about how women are naturally on a higher spiritual plane than men, and thus don't need to engage in the kind of learning men do. And even if most of the women in his family seem to accept this logic—indeed embrace it, expressing their relief at not having to study—he himself cannot abide it. In fact, Yitzchak wishes that he could convince his mother not to abide it, either. He thinks she is the smartest member of the family by far, and that she secretly longs to go to school.

Yitzchak remembers once asking his father why, on Shabbos, he always cut off the end of the *challah* and gave it to his mother. Assuming that it was probably because his mother liked crusty bread, he was horrified to learn that there is actually a superstition that eating the edge of the challah causes people to become forgetful. Yitzchak interpreted his father's act as an implicit endorsement of the view that, while a man surely cannot risk forgetting all that he has learned, there is little serious harm that could come to a woman from losing a bit of her memory. "After all, what does a woman know?" Yitzchak asks me, rolling his eyes, "A few recipes, maybe, or how to wash the floor?"

Yitzchak knows that, within the context of his family, his father is a genuinely loving and caring man, who also has a deep respect for his mother. But he also sees that his father has internalized the community's approach to women more generally. This became strikingly clear to Yitzchak during a discussion in which his father claimed he saw nothing offensive about the idea that, in a Jewish court, the testimony of a mentally ill man would be accepted over that of a perfectly sane woman. Indeed, it makes Yitzchak both angry and sad that women in his community don't receive the same encouragement that men do to engage in intellectual pursuits—although in the Hasidic world even men are not encouraged to pursue anything beyond religious learning, save for practical training in order to make a living.

Unlike the many Orthodox feminists whose work he has read, Yitzchak doesn't think that most Hasidic women really long to study Talmud, or to lead services. The fundamental problem, he would argue, is that the community shuns intellectual involvement in anything outside of religion. And given that that avenue is closed to women, there are practically no outlets for female intellectual curiosity. At least in Lubavitch, the women participate in religious outreach, answering questions and helping others to learn, which can be intellectually challenging.

Quite apart from being denied intellectual stimulation, most women in the community, according to Yitzchak, rarely, if ever, get to experience the kind of joy men do—and with which Hasidism is so romantically associated. While men are out at shul, or eating and singing at their rebbe's *tish*, or table, on Friday nights, their wives, daughters, and sisters are home recovering from their Sabbath preparations and putting children to bed. And it's the same thing when men are dancing on *Simchas Torah*, or drinking and carousing on Purim. To Yitzchak, the worst part of all this is that Hasidic philosophy "is very tolerant of others and women, an antinomian philosophy, without the obsession with laws" that has come to define communities like his own.

Today, while Yitzchak still lives in his community and wears the Hasidic garb when he goes out in the area (mostly for the sake of his daughters and his parents), he tries not to let it get to him anymore. Thinking about it too much makes his blood pressure rise. He no longer teaches the men, working instead in the day school full-time. He would still call himself religious—simply not on the community's terms.

For a long time, it was hard for Yitzchak to separate the communal and behavioral practices his parents had taught him from everything else about the religion, but it has grown easier. Now he keeps the commandments that have meaning for him, and in terms of his observance, he is basically a modern Orthodox Jew, although he doesn't identify with this group on an emotional level. After all, he didn't grow up in modern Orthodox circles, and, despite his criticisms of the Hasidic community, he acknowledges his emotional ties to certain aspects of Hasidic culture. In fact, Yitzchak's experience seems to suggest that religious practice, or even belief, is not the exclusive determinant of a person's religious identity. The culture of one's religious *community* plays an important part as well.

Yitzchak knows that in a great many ways he has been extremely lucky. He knows about people who left and were completely rejected by their families, but his parents were always tolerant of, if not exactly happy about, his intellectual explorations and iconoclastic views. Of course, there were many times over the years when his father came to him and asked whether he really needed to do so much reading, whether he had done enough and could now, finally, do without it. And he still asks him these questions today. But Yitzchak's parents have never condemned or rejected him, and for that he is grateful. Indeed, his scholarly achievements within the community —which may have been his unconscious way of softening the blow— have made Yitzchak's parents extremely proud.

It's not all perfect, of course. Recently he began dating, although only modern Orthodox women, who he believes may have at least some sense of where he's coming from. This has been very difficult for his parents, who still want to see him end up with a woman who will cover her hair after marriage and wear only dresses and skirts. In fact, they are hoping that when (not *if*) he remarries, he won't have mixed seating at his wedding, as it goes against their Hasidic values. But Yitzchak keeps explaining to them that although he has chosen to live differently from them, his is not a valueless life. Indeed, to Yitzchak, mixed seating is an important value in itself, the value of equality.

Like his parents, Yitzchak's daughters also know everything about his life these days. He has made a big effort to make them understand that he didn't "rebel just for the sake of rebelling," but out of conviction, and that he will respect whatever choices they make in their lives, as well. For now, however, the girls seem to be happy in the community, with their own friends and immersed in their familiar routines. This isn't to say that they are not in some measure confused, but, in the end, Yitzchak believes that their confusion can be a good thing. It makes them think. In fact, whenever he is out with his daughters and they drive past a non-Hasidic couple holding hands or embracing, Yitzchak always makes sure they take a good look. Expressing passion and affection for another person isn't immodest, he wants them to know; it is an essential part of being human.

So now Yitzchak is no longer a rock star in his community, although at times he has fantasized about doing something worthy of one: getting a tattoo—which he would never actually do, because it is against Jewish law. The support for this prohibition is in Leviticus 19:28, which states: "You shall not make gashes in your flesh for the dead, or incise any marks on yourself: I am the Lord." Traditional Judaism understands the body not as something over which an individual has ultimate control, but rather as a temporary house for his or her soul, on loan from God. Defacing the body is like an insult to God's generosity.

Even though Yitzchak knows he won't ever be visiting a tattoo parlor, he thinks the idea once held so much appeal for him because he was raised with so many rules and restrictions related to his body. Growing up, he was told what kind of food he could put into his body and when, and how he had to clothe it. He was instructed on the proper times and methods to wash its various parts, and even made to restrain its activities on certain days, lest his body be engaged in something that someone else defined as work. He was also required to grow a beard, whether he wanted to have one or not. And, most difficult of all, Yitzchak felt he had no control over how, when, and with whom he could use his body for pleasure, or to express love, passion, friendship, or joy.

Of course, even living as a modern Orthodox Jew, he is still subject to many of these same restrictions, particularly the laws related to food and the prohibition against work on the Sabbath. But there is more diversity and less rigidity in the modern Orthodox world. And because this life is something that Yitzchak feels he has chosen, rather than having it imposed on him without his consent, his body no longer feels as if it's under anyone's control but his own. With that realization, the desire to assert control over it by drawing on it has disappeared—although Yitzchak is still enough of an aesthete (all of that time sneaking off to museums wasn't wasted on him) to appreciate a beautiful tattoo whenever he sees one on somebody else.

Chapter Nine

Dancing at Two Weddings

There is something very wrong with Yossi. At least that's what his grandmother is telling Malkie Schwartz over her cell phone, as Malkie and I sit together drinking iced coffees at a Greek café in her Queens neighborhood. It's a humid summer Friday afternoon and, after a sticky subway ride from Manhattan, Malkie and I are relieved to be in the air conditioning. We are not relieved, however, to have received this call.

According to his grandmother, Yossi has been very jittery for the past few days, unable to sit still, or eat, or even speak in anything approaching a coherent sentence. One minute he will be pacing inside her house, only to dart outside the next, disappearing for short stretches of time before running back in through the front door. Whenever she asks him what's going on, he just stammers and starts the whole bizarre process all over again. She has already tried to reach a doctor who treats people in the community, but because it's Friday, only a few hours before the beginning of Shabbos, the doctor, who is Orthodox, has already left his office. Since she knows that Yossi has been attending some of Malkie's programs, she figured she would try to call her, and took her number off Yossi's cell phone. When she learns that I am here with Malkie, she asks to speak to me, too.

After a few minutes, it becomes clear that Yossi's grandmother wants the two of us to come into Brooklyn to see him. She thinks that maybe he will talk to us about what's bothering him. She is very concerned, she tells us, but we should also understand that she is not a young woman anymore, and she is not sure she can handle this on her own. Yossi's father, in fact his whole family, is up in the mountains, but, given the recent history, his grandmother doesn't think that calling them would be such a good idea. Her daughter has promised her that she will try to stop by later, but with it being Shabbos, everyone is busy making their preparations. It would be a great help to her if we came, she says. And if we do, of course she will have plenty of food.

I tell Yossi's grandmother that we will call her back in a few minutes, giving us some time to figure out what to do. We are not sure how we might actually be able to help Yossi—neither of us is a doctor or a psychologist, after all—but the situation does sound pretty bad, and at this point Malkie is certainly no stranger to these kinds of emergency calls. In fact, her work has required her to develop a network of psychiatrists, social workers, and physicians, some of whom she can try to call. While none of these professionals is religious, a Friday afternoon in high summer is hardly the easiest time to reach anyone in New York.

Then there is the matter of how we are dressed. Both of us are wearing t-shirts and jeans, not exactly appropriate attire for a visit to a Hasidic community, let alone a Hasidic home; our arrival would certainly prompt stares and gossip from the neighbors. Malkie could go home and change, she suggests unconvincingly. She could even lend me something to wear, if I want. But the mere thought of putting on stockings and a long skirt and long-sleeved shirt right now is unbearable, given the heat. If we are going to go, we decide, we will go as we are. The neighbors will have to deal with it.

Malkie and I quickly finish our drinks, and she calls Yossi's grandmother back to tell her that we are on our way. Getting to Brooklyn from Queens on the subway can be a convoluted nightmare, so we decide to call a car service to take us there instead. Traffic is at a crawl, but with a humid haze blanketing the Brooklyn-Queens Expressway, we are only grateful that the car is air-conditioned. Malkie takes out her cell phone and begins leaving messages for all of her various doctors and therapists. We hope someone will still be in the office to return the call.

Whatever's going on with Yossi, we are not exactly surprised that something like this has happened. For several months now, he has been making sometimes multiple daily trips back and forth between Brooklyn and Manhattan at all hours, often changing his clothes on the subway, or in the bathrooms of bars and nightclubs, and even the Museum of Television and Radio. He has begun spending a lot of time there, in a comfortable private cubicle, watching old episodes of *The Goldbergs*—a show that originated as a skit in the Catskills, became a radio program, then moved to TV in 1949, chronicling one immigrant Jewish family's journey of assimilation into the American middle class. Yossi has even bought a membership to the museum, allowing him unlimited time at the monitors and reduced-price access to all kinds of special lectures and presentations. When he is done with *The Goldbergs*, he plans to take a look at all of *The Odd Couple* episodes he has missed in reruns.

And he has also been drinking. A lot. Not just Joeys anymore, but his favorite new discovery, the Long Island Iced Tea—a combination of five different kinds of alcohol (vodka, gin, triple sec, rum, and tequila), but no tea to speak of. The drink is perfect for Yossi because he can feel its effects after having just one, which is a real money saver for someone on a tight budget. Yossi claims he likes to drink because it loosens him up and makes it easier for him to talk to girls in bars. It also gives him the courage to do other kinds of things, such as making an impromptu visit to a hookah parlor in a Muslim section of Queens, wearing his shtreimel and bekishe. Fortunately, most of the Egyptian hookah smokers seemed genuinely intrigued to see him there, and Yossi still likes to think of that foray as his personal contribution to the effort to bring about peace in the Middle East.

But he also finds that alcohol can make him very emotional. Often, when he is drunk, he ends up thinking about his family—about his parents, and how all they can do is tell him what a terrible disappointment he is and warn him to stay away from the house and the other children. And sometimes he ends up locking himself in the bathroom of wherever he happens to be and crying uncontrollably. A few times, bartenders have gotten concerned enough to ask him to leave, and he has spent the rest of the night hunched over on a stoop somewhere until the sun comes up and he is sober enough to find his way back to his grandmother's house.

Needless to say, Yossi might not do so much late-night drinking if he actually had something to get up for in the morning. He has been trying to find a job, putting in applications at neighborhood stores, mostly places selling hardware, electronics, or men's clothing. He even inquired at a plant that manufactures *tallisim*, or prayer shawls. It is a place where he once worked as a teenager, becoming terribly depressed by the tedious work and factory-like conditions. But so far, nobody has offered him anything, a demoralizing situation that has certainly been a factor in all the drinking. Yossi is aware that he probably doesn't come off very well in these job interviews, mainly because he can't muster the appropriate enthusiasm for the work. He also suspects that by now the word about him has reached everyone in the community, and that most people are probably just wary of having him around. He finds this particularly ironic, since he regrew the beard and peyos precisely because his father convinced him that doing so might allay people's concerns and make the whole episode look like some immature act of rebellion. Even all of Yossi's potential tutoring customers (the pyromaniac included) are out of town, attending summer camps up in the mountains.

So, for the past many months, Yossi has had to finance his trips into the city mostly by relying on small handouts from his grandmother and the proceeds from his infrequent Judaica deals. Recently, however, he has talked about selling some big-ticket items. He has a very valuable set of tefillin, which he believes he could move pretty quickly, and there is also his shtreimel, which he would rather not part with, but which could probably bring in close to two thousand dollars, as it is made out of mink tails. Every man in Yossi's community gets a shtreimel when he marries, and it is customary to wear them out on Shabbos and holidays. There was once a time when only the most pious men would wear a shtreimel. But now, according to Yossi, "every schmuck puts one on" on Friday night, diluting its meaning and undermining people's ability to identify the most devout members of the community. This turn of events has actually made things easier for Yossi, as he has figured out how to hide important items, like his cell phone, under his shtreimel when he decides to sneak out of the community on Shabbos.

Of course, Yossi has also thought about shaving off his beard again in the hope that a more modern look will increase his chances of finding work outside the community. But after what happened last year with the Yiddishists, he has been wary of doing it. He now understands that, unless he wants to pump gas or work in a cell phone store, like some of the people he has met through Malkie's programs, finding work on the outside will not be easy. Of course, it's not that Yossi doesn't think he has the ability to pump gas or sign people up for cell phone service. He is just very nervous that his unfamiliarity with the secular world will cause him to make a stupid mistake, and he'll be yelled at by an angry boss. It's because of fears like this that school was always easier for him than work. Even though it was difficult to have to pretend to believe in things he didn't, as long as he did well, nobody bothered him there.

In fact, for a while this spring, Yossi had actually been talking about applying to Brooklyn College. His interest in going to college had been piqued by a "field trip" that he, Malkie, and I took to visit the National Yiddish Book Center in Amherst, Massachusetts. The Center was founded in 1980 by a man named Aaron Lansky who, as a young graduate student, discovered that across North America thousands of Yiddish books that had survived both Hitler and Stalin were now being discarded and destroyed. An entire literature was on the verge of extinction, as the children and grandchildren of a dying generation literally threw out the volumes, unable to read the language.

Lansky took a leave from graduate school and put out a public call for unwanted Yiddish books. People responded. Before long, Lansky and a group of coworkers were hitting the road, retrieving Jewish books from basements and attics, as well as synagogues, abandoned buildings, and even dumpsters. When Lansky first began his campaign, scholars estimated that there were about seventy thousand extant Yiddish books to be recovered. The Center ended up collecting that many in only six months. Today, the place boasts over 1.5 million volumes and is still receiving more books each week. While the Center keeps the first copy of every book it receives, and sends the second on to the Library of Congress in Washington, any additional copies are available for sale at a modest price, the goal being to get as many of these books back into circulation and the hands of readers as possible. A grant from Steven Spielberg is enabling the Center to digitize its entire collection, making reprints of its volumes available on demand.

While Yossi had long known about the Center, he had never had a chance to visit it. In fact, he had never traveled *anywhere* outside of New York or New Jersey. So, when one of Malkie's friends in Northampton offered to put us all up for a night, Yossi jumped at the chance to come along. During the car ride up to Massachusetts, he was like a little kid. He was full of excitement, pointing out all sorts of things on the road that I was too jaded to experience as new or even remotely interesting. Sometimes his enthusiasm caused him to perceive novelty where it seemed unlikely—when he declared, for example, that the trees in Connecticut, only about fifty miles north of Manhattan, looked "completely different" from the trees in New York and New Jersey. But then again, maybe they did.

When we arrived in Northampton, Yossi was stunned. This was a "real *shtetl*," a town with a busy, wide main street lined with storefronts and filled with young people. Yossi thought the place even looked a little like some parts of Brooklyn, "but in the country." He was thrilled to learn that there were so many colleges in the area, and intrigued to discover that this was also a town that was particularly hospitable to gay people. Having changed in the car into Stan's jeans, a blue t-shirt, and a bandanna, he was also thrilled to notice that, in terms of his appearance at least, he seemed to fit right in.

His behavior, however, was another story. The minute we got

out of the car, Yossi began singing "Born Free" at the top of his lungs, and skipping down the street. At one point he suggested, rather loudly in a coffeehouse, after one of Malkie's friends had asked him whether he was kosher, that he get a t-shirt made for himself that read: "I eat everything, and I fuck everything." When Malkie told him that such a message might be open to all kinds of misinterpretation, for a while Yossi seemed genuinely puzzled as to why that would be the case. Wasn't it a great thing to be open to everything and everyone? Wasn't that the true spirit of a liberal, which he unequivocally was? Wasn't it because of this attitude that he was supposed to heed the demands of all those bumper stickers we saw on the way up and vote for John Kerry, unlike the rest of his community, who would, as usual, follow the rebbe's instructions and cast their votes for Bush?

By the time we made it to the Yiddish Book Center, Yossi had calmed down a little, although he couldn't completely contain his "joy" at being "in wonderful Massachusetts." As we were approaching the Book Center, Yossi rolled down his window and, in an exaggerated Yiddish accent worthy of the worst productions of *Fiddler on the Roof*, asked two preppy-looking women who were holding hands if they "by any chance knew where the *tren* station was." When, quite understandably, they assumed he was looking for the train station, and began to offer detailed directions to it, Yossi started to laugh uncontrollably. Apparently he'd thought that the women, walking so close to the Yiddish Book Center, surely knew that *tren* was Yiddish slang for "fuck." Wouldn't they fly into hysterics to hear someone asking directions to the "fuck station"? Obviously not. As we apologized to the bewildered women and drove off, we had to explain to Yossi that, despite the proximity of the Yiddish Book Center, it was unlikely that either of these women was fluent in Yiddish slang. We weren't, after all, in Brooklyn anymore.

Of course, Yossi was completely enthralled by the Center, combing its stacks for books to purchase, and photocopying excerpts from those he couldn't afford to buy. He even found a poem written by a

Hasidic man in the 1860s, describing what it felt like the first time he shaved his beard. Yossi was amazed to discover that, in addition to their modern inclinations, he and the writer also shared the same last name. It was clear that Yossi would have stayed among the books until closing time if we hadn't extracted him to go get dinner.

Later that night, Yossi went out to explore Northampton on his own, checking out the various nightspots and even taking in a cheap movie at the local theater. When he got back to the house, he stayed up until 4:00 a.m. watching MTV for the very first time in his life. He was totally captivated by how "crazy and loose" all the rock stars were. The next day, as we toured the campuses of Smith and the University of Massachusetts, he couldn't stop going on about what "a dream" it would be to be a rock star, or at least appear on TV.

When Yossi got back to New York, he was very excited about the prospect of going to college. When it actually came time to channel his excitement into concrete action, however, Yossi became paralyzed. How was he going to get financial aid to pay for school? What if he couldn't do the work, never having written a paper or taken a written exam before? What if the other students thought he was a loser? And then there was the whole issue of not having a real transcript to send to the admissions office. All of these questions became so overwhelming that, even after he took the bus out to tour the Brooklyn College campus, Yossi was still too nervous to talk to someone in the admissions office, or even to call for an application. He didn't even know how to write an application essay.

Malkie had offered to work with Yossi on all of this, as she had done for others. She was even beginning to develop a formal program to help people prepare for the GED exam. But sometimes Yossi was too embarrassed to accept even Malkie's help, fearing that she would quickly discover what he already believed about himself: that he couldn't succeed at college. Yossi knew that to some people it would appear that he was just lazy, not interested in making the effort. And maybe there was some truth to that. But a big part of his reluctance had to do with the fact that he had grown up with so many rules and restrictions, with people telling him what to do all the time. Yossi no longer wanted to take orders or instructions from anybody. He wanted to be his own person. And he wanted to be famous, so that people would like him automatically, and he could do whatever he wanted.

When Malkie and I finally arrive in Yossi's neighborhood, the pre-Shabbos bustle has all but disappeared. The stores are now shuttered, and the streets are almost empty, save for the occasional Hasidic man buying a bouquet from one of the many Latino vendors who set up temporary shop on Friday afternoons, their shopping carts filled with bunches of flowers. It is something of a tradition for Hasidic husbands to bring their wives flowers on shabbos, and apparently the custom has created a secure niche for these outside vendors. It is still somewhat disconcerting to see them here, however, a colorful touch of Latin America on the black-and-white streets of Eastern Europe.

When we get to Yossi's grandmother's house, we ring the bell and she quickly lets us in. Yossi appears at the door behind her like a ghost. He looks as if he has lost ten pounds and, even with a belt, his black pants are slipping down below his waist. He can barely muster the energy to greet either of us, and, as soon as we get inside the house, he disappears into another room, only to reemerge a few minutes later with an odd grin on his face. Like some kind of Borscht Belt M.C., he tells us that he is happy we made it here tonight, that it is good to see us, and then, as if nothing were amiss, he invites us to go out to a bar with him. We gingerly point out that it's Shabbos, not exactly a time for going out to bars, but he doesn't seem to care.

"I am not letting you go anywhere," his grandmother declares, and the grin suddenly disappears from his face. He begins to plead with her. She is resolute. "And it's not because it's Shabbos. I already know what you do on shabbos. I'm not letting you out because you're in no condition to leave this house. The girls can stay here with you."

Suddenly, I feel as if Malkie and I have accidentally boarded a plane for the wrong destination, and it's now taxiing down the runway, about to take off. I glance at Malkie, and her expression seems to reflect my own mounting concern. Stay here? No way. There is some commotion outside the front door, and several men, all Yossi's relatives, appear in the foyer. They are on their way to shul. Yossi's grandmother goes to the door to speak to them, leaving us with Yossi, who is now rocking back and forth in a chair at the large dining room table.

We ask him if he can tell us what's bothering him, and he mumbles something about being very nervous and about needing to go outside. He has these urges, these compulsions, he says, that force him to go back to places over and over again. "I'm very scared," he says, before burying his head in his hands.

Yossi's grandmother returns and begins talking to us about what she calls his "shtick." Apparently, since he was a little child, Yossi has had some form of obsessive-compulsive disorder that causes him to ruminate about certain things and, when it gets very bad, to return over and over again to the scenes of various "crimes"—places where bad things happened to him—so that he can "undo" the negative experiences. But this kind of thing hasn't happened to him in a long time, she explains, and she doesn't know why it's happening now.

"Maybe it's this ridiculous way you are living," she says to Yossi, who is now staring at the floor. "Back and forth, and here and there, in and out of the clothes. You know the saying," she says. "With one tuchus, you can't dance at two weddings."

"I know," Yossi says quietly.

"Maybe it's enough already," she says with a shrug.

It is hard to tell exactly what Yossi's grandmother means by this. Does she think that it's time for Yossi to stop running around and stay put, here in the community? Or does she think he just needs to make a choice, whatever choice he truly wants? It's hard to tell. She is playing it close to the vest.

Yossi gets up from his chair and heads for the front door again.

By now, it has grown dark outside, and Shabbos, which will last until sundown tomorrow evening, is officially under way, heralded a few minutes earlier by the Shabbos horn. Malkie and I decide to follow Yossi outside. When he sees us, he turns around and comes back into the house. Just then, Malkie's phone rings. For a split second, a look of panic crosses her face. It is forbidden to use the phone on Shabbos, and even though Malkie has not been observant for several years, she nonetheless remains highly attuned to religious protocol. Yossi's grandmother doesn't seem to react to this breach. Indeed, it is then that I realize that Malkie and I were probably summoned here, even perhaps unconsciously, as Shabbos goyim, non-Jews to whom the laws of Sabbath observance don't apply.

The Shabbos goy has an important history in Judaism; throughout time, observant Jews have made use of the services of non-Jews to carry out necessary activities prohibited on the Sabbath. As with most things in Jewish law, the regulations pertaining to the use of a Shabbos goy are quite complex (whether or not the observant Jew can request his services directly, for example), but the allowance for such a person nonetheless offers religious Jews one way (among several others) to circumvent certain Sabbath prohibitions, if need be.[1] Although, technically, "goy" refers to a non-Jew, in this case, Malkie and I certainly fill the bill.

It turns out that the caller is a therapist, responding to one of Malkie's messages. After hearing about what's been going on with Yossi, she suggests that we get him to a hospital immediately. Maimonides, which she says has a good psychiatric department, is nearby, and she thinks it would be best to bring him to the emergency room there. Yossi's grandmother seems to take the news with relief. Her daughter, who arrives a few minutes later, however, does not. We can't lock him up in a hospital, she tells us. What if they do something to his brain, like give it a shock, and he becomes a vegetable? Maybe he won't get good care there. Maybe we should take him to a hospital in the city? What if someone from the community sees him there and thinks he is a crazy? What then?

We get nowhere. We offer to call the therapist back, but neither of the women will violate the Sabbath and talk to her on the phone. While we are trying to make a decision about what to do, Yossi bounces from room to room like a pinball, tugging on his beard. When he overhears his aunt mention electroshock, he runs into the kitchen where we are sitting and insists that he isn't going anywhere. His aunt looks victorious. His grandmother looks exhausted.

After an hour and a half more of this, we finally tell Yossi's grandmother that we are going to have to leave. It is growing late, and we both need to get home. She looks stricken. Yossi's aunt is still here —probably the only thing, in her mind, standing between Yossi and five hundred volts—and she is not budging an inch. Maybe, we suggest again, they should speak directly with the doctor. After all, isn't this the kind of emergency for which one is allowed to violate the Sabbath?

Not exactly. Apparently, it is only a clear call when it's a matter of life or death. For this situation, they would need to consult a rabbi, which they couldn't do now anyway because it's Shabbos, and, of course, he wouldn't answer his phone. The circularity of this argument only serves to exacerbate Malkie's and my growing sense of frustration. It feels as if we are fiddling while Yossi burns. Maybe we could walk to the rabbi's house, I suggest. I get no response. I sense there is an invisible battle being waged here between what's best for Yossi in the short term (seeing a doctor) and what's best for the family in the long term (keeping this unfortunate episode from the community), and the long term is winning out.

Malkie and I finally make our move toward the door, and in that moment, Yossi's grandmother suddenly gives in, or up, or out. She is overruling her daughter. She cannot be responsible for Yossi all weekend. She has no energy left.

While Malkie and I usher Yossi to the door, his grandmother tells us that we shouldn't try to hail a cab to the hospital until we are several blocks away from her house, on the outskirts of the neighborhood, where nobody will recognize Yossi, as it is also forbidden to travel in a car on Shabbos. And when we come back, we should be sure to ask the cab driver to stop a few blocks from the house and walk us to the door, so that nobody sees Yossi getting out of a car on Shabbos, either. Apparently, it doesn't matter whether God—for whom Yossi is supposedly keeping these commandments—notices that he is taking a cab. As usual, it's the neighbors we have to be concerned about.

Because she cannot handle money on Shabbos, Yossi's grandmother assures us that if we lay out the money for the cab fare, she will pay us back on Sunday. She also tells us that Yossi can give us the combination to the door lock (it is also forbidden to carry anything—a house key included—on Shabbos), so that if he needs to be at the hospital overnight, we can at least come back to the house and let ourselves in to tell her what's going on. Until sundown tomorrow night, she also won't be able to answer the phone.

Getting Yossi into a cab turns out to be much easier said than done. He can barely walk. He has almost no energy, as he hasn't eaten in several days, and he is so anxious about being outside that he can't take more than a few steps before stopping to insist that we turn around and go back to his grandmother's house. We keep telling him that this is not a good idea, that we are taking him to the hospital, where they will be able to make him feel better, but that he must walk with us. He asks whether we can go down a different block because there is a house coming up that he is very nervous about passing. In fact, he tells us, the whole street is "contaminated."

Malkie and I are too drained to indulge this request, and instead we each grab one of his arms and begin literally to drag him down the street. We are still in the Hasidic section of the neighborhood, and the few people we pass who are out taking after-Shabbos-dinner strolls can't help but stare at us. Nobody knows what to make of this Hasidic man who is being led down the street—touched even—by two *shiksas* in jeans. So much for keeping this from the neighbors.

The minute we walk through the doors of the emergency room, Yossi seems almost back to his old self. Indeed, it appears that the relief of knowing that he is going to get some help has calmed him down enough so that he can actually sit and watch CNN on the TV blaring above us. The emergency room is pretty crowded—there are even a few Hasidic families there—and the nurse at the window tells we are going to have a wait. By about one in the morning, a doctor takes Yossi in to be examined. One of the nurses offers him something to eat. She assures him that the food here is kosher—Maimonides is a Jewish hospital, after all—and Yossi gives us a sly smile as he bites into a peanut butter sandwich, the first thing he has eaten all day. Before long, he is cracking jokes with the staff.

The doctor wants to admit Yossi to the psychiatric ward for a few days, for observation. He seems to think that this is a flare-up of the old obsessive-compulsive disorder, probably in response to all the stress Yossi has been under, trying to manage his two lives. But he also thinks Yossi could use some therapy as well. Working in this neighborhood, he explains, he has seen many Hasidic people in Yossi's position, and he seems to understand the situation well. He also tells us that it is going to be a while before they find Yossi a bed, so we will have to be patient.

Malkie agrees to stay with Yossi until they can admit him, letting me off the hook to take myself home to bed. In the cab back to Manhattan, my cell phone rings. It is almost 3:00 a.m. I answer the phone, and a little boy's voice replies on the other end of the line. It is Yossi's cousin, who is seven. He has been awakened by his mother to dial and hold the phone, which, I am later told, is OK, because a young child who violates the Sabbath cannot be held accountable for it like an adult. I tell Yossi's aunt that he is going to be admitted for a few days and that he seems much better already. She thanks me and hangs up. At 6:30 I get another call, although this time the little boy is holding the phone up to Yossi's grandmother's ear. It seems the child got just about as much sleep as I did that night.

On Sunday, Malkie and I go back to visit Yossi in the hospital. The ward is crowded, though hardly bustling, its inhabitants mostly sitting idly, bathed in fluorescent light and the aroma of institutional food. Yossi does not seem exactly happy to see us, although he is no longer so agitated. They have him on something for the anxiety, he tells us, and his grandmother, aunt, and he are supposed to meet with a social worker tomorrow. He thinks he will be able to get some therapy here, and also a recommendation for someone to see once he gets out. The hospital has some groups he can attend during the day, as an outpatient. It's weird and a little boring being in this place, he says, but he feels much calmer.

Yossi's grandmother arrives shortly after we do, loaded down with a shopping bag full of Yossi's favorite foods: cholent left over from Shabbos, pickled herring, some challah, and gefilte fish. In no time, she is schmoozing with the other patients in the common room—a skinny Asian, a heavyset religious woman wearing a wig, a tall Jamaican woman with colorful beads in her braided hair—and offering them food. It doesn't seem to bother her in the least that these people are all psychiatric patients. Nobody here seems violent or crazy. "Who doesn't have problems?" she says matter-of-factly. "They could still be hungry for good food." Her greatest sympathy seems to extend to a young woman who has apparently recently become religious, and is also more than a little unhinged—which Yossi's grandmother does not see as a coincidence. To her mind, sudden religious zealotry is often a sign that "something's not right." And, as if on cue to prove her point, the young woman spends the next half hour asking everyone on the ward, over and over again, whether they have a prayer book she could borrow, and also if they might be interested in starting a home business.

After an hour or so, Yossi warms up to us a little, and he and his grandmother also begin to talk about what to tell his father. Yossi is terrified that his father may find out about this episode, but his grandmother reveals that the family is planning to return home on Wednesday, three days from now. As long as Yossi is out of the hospital by then, his grandmother says, his father need never know any of this ever happened. Yossi remembers one of the staff members telling him that he might need to be here for a week in order to be properly evaluated. Suddenly he realizes this will mean his father could find out, and he decides he will tell the social worker that he wants to leave tomorrow.

His grandmother begins to back-pedal, telling him that he shouldn't be so worried about his father, that he should do whatever he needs to do to get better. And then Yossi asks her about his aunt. What does she think he should do? he wants to know. Yossi's grandmother insists that what his aunt thinks doesn't matter, either. But Yossi knows she probably wants him out of here as well, if only so that her children won't be tainted by having a cousin in a nuthouse. It seems the only opinion he doesn't want to figure out is his own.

On Monday afternoon, I call the hospital to find that Yossi has checked out.

Chapter Ten

A Cautionary Tale

Dressed in black pants and a tailored leather jacket, her pretty face framed by shoulder-length, golden-brown hair and a pair of funky, black-rimmed glasses, Leah looks as if she would fit in perfectly at a gallery opening in Chelsea, or maybe a pool hall in the East Village. Indeed, it is hard to believe that she is the person in the photograph I am holding: a young woman dressed in a long, shapeless housedress, her shaved head covered with a scarf, a newborn cradled in her arms. But if you ask Leah, she will tell you that the woman in the picture was just a very good actress, maybe one worthy of an Academy Award. Indeed, she will say that the person she is today was really always there, beneath the scarf and the dress, just waiting for a way to get out. Leah will also tell you that the person in the picture is much healthier and happier these days, now that she isn't acting anymore. But that certainly didn't happen without a fight.

Leah was born and raised in the Satmar community of Williamsburg, the third oldest of eleven children. From the time she was a little girl, she was always asking questions, curious about everything and everyone around her. A little too curious, in fact, by the standards of her community, which had very strict rules about what one could do, and with whom one could do it. For example, even though Leah knew it was immodest, she still liked to run around outside on the street and play with boys, chasing them, or throwing things at them from behind parked cars when they weren't looking. She didn't like it that she always had to wear skirts, especially because it made it harder to run fast and catch the boys. And Leah also didn't like it when people told her how much she should be looking forward to growing up and getting married, to shaving her head and covering it with a tichel, or scarf, just like her mother did. The truth was, even then she knew she never wanted to wear a tichel. She hated the way it looked.

Leah was often punished, or beaten, for her "wild" behavior, and also for doing things like talking to people who weren't Jewish and from the community—people like the nice Italian plumber, or the friendly black guy who delivered packages for UPS. It wasn't that Leah was trying to make trouble. It was just that she wanted to know what different kinds of people were like, and also to get a little positive attention from someone, for a change. And maybe, deep down, Leah also felt that hearing about other people's lives might help her forget, if only temporarily, about the troubles of her own.

Take, for example, the fact that she had been molested repeatedly by a man in the community when she was just ten years old. Although Leah told only her closest friends about it, somehow the story got back to her school principal, who reported it to her parents and then promptly expelled her, claiming that she would be a bad influence on the other students. As if this weren't punishment enough, Leah's father then threatened to burn her with a hot pan if she ever spoke up about the molestation to anyone again. From then on, when she wasn't "in a total daze," as she puts it, Leah was consumed by confusion and fear.

In fact, according to Leah, in the house where she grew up, everything was "based on fear." If she did something against the rules, even by accident, she was immediately threatened with going to hell. Performing the commandments was never about expressing gratitude to God, or love, or joy, but only about fear. If she forgot to make a blessing over her food, for example, she got a smack. And the same thing happened if she was caught reading a secular book, or if she didn't keep her hair in braids, as she was supposed to.

Sometimes Leah even ended up in the emergency room, covered with injuries from her mother's beatings, which she told the nurses came from falling down the stairs. She was apparently a good enough actress even then that the nurses believed her, or at least wanted to. Eventually, even family outings that should have been fun, such as going once a year to see the animals at the zoo, filled Leah with terror. There were so many things on the street she wasn't allowed to look at, like couples holding hands, or immodest clothing displayed in store windows, that it got to the point where she actually preferred to stay at home.

When she was about sixteen, Leah befriended a girl from her neighborhood who, it turned out, had a TV and VCR hidden in her house. Soon enough, Leah was sneaking over to her new friend's apartment to watch videos. The first movie she ever saw was *Mrs. Doubtfire,* a comedy in which Robin Williams spends half the movie in drag, dressed as an English nanny. For Leah, seeing the film was "total culture shock." In a world with such rigid gender roles, where all men dressed alike and it was a sin for a woman to wear pants, the movie might just as well have been a *National Geographic* documentary about life on Mars. Other films followed, however, and soon Leah was "glued."

Around the same time, Leah also became involved in a relationship with her boss, a married Hasidic man from the community who was in his forties. She worked part-time as a secretary in his real estate business, and whenever he passed by her desk, he would "accidentally" bump up against her. Sometimes when she returned from the bathroom, there would be a condom sitting on her chair. Her boss also liked to tell Leah how cute she was, and, in time, he exposed her to a lot of explicit sexual material. Because she had been going along with it, Leah knew she could never tell anyone about the situation. If word got out, the man would surely deny everything, and she would, once again, take all the blame and all the punishment. Although, in her heart, Leah knew the whole situation was terribly wrong, she also couldn't help enjoying the attention. It was certainly more than she ever got at home.

In fact, Leah's home life was filled with a tremendous amount of work and responsibility. She was often left to take care of her younger siblings while her mother went off for several weeks to visit her own relatives in other parts of the country. With little help from her two older brothers, Leah would cook and clean and diaper and bathe, all unwelcome preparation for her inevitable life to come.

Then, when she was seventeen, Leah agreed to get engaged. Even though she met the boy only once before the wedding, for about forty-five minutes, Leah decided to marry him because she just wanted so badly to get out of her parents' house.

Of course, looking back, Leah now wishes that she had been able to get to know the boy better, but she also knows that her parents would never have let her date in a way that allowed that. It would have been nice to take the time to see whether they were compatible, or could maybe even fall in love. But nobody in the community did that. You got married and that was it. As far as being ready was concerned, "you didn't need to know more than how to cook, clean, wash, stay at home and take care of the kids and be a good wife." To even talk about marrying for love would have provoked her parents' anger. They would have accused her of thinking she was a goy and then punished her for the thought.

So, Leah got married and, in the beginning at least, tried hard to make the marriage work, shaving her head and covering it, as her mother had, dressing the part and preparing nice meals and keeping the house clean. She tried to convince herself that what she had learned in school was true, that even though she hated the way she looked and the way she was spending her time, all these sacrifices actually brought her closer to God. But, as much as she repeated this to herself, it never really worked. She just got better at pretending.

Leah's husband was a good person, as it turned out, and he treated her nicely. But, like her, he was also from an emotionally troubled background, and Leah now understands that neither of them had any idea how to have a "normal" relationship with another person. But because her husband wasn't a fanatic—he didn't tell her what to do, or hit her, or threaten her with going to hell—for the first time in her life, Leah calmed down. She calmed down enough, over time, to realize that this was not the life she wanted for herself. She didn't "feel connected" to the things she was doing, never really liked any of it, and couldn't imagine going on with a life of faking and hiding. However, by that time she had already had her daughter, and the idea of leaving had become a lot more complicated. But still, she knew she had to get out. She just had no idea how, and no one to turn to.

And so, for several years, Leah didn't do anything too drastic. She did, however, stop shaving her head, hiding her short hair under her tichel instead. She also bought herself a computer and signed up for an account with AOL. She started surfing the Web and reading up on religion in general, and Judaism in particular. Eventually, she began talking to people in Jewish chat rooms and realizing that there was "a whole world outside where people lead normal lives and have the freedom to be who they are." In one chat room, she even befriended a modern Orthodox woman from the Upper West Side, and soon the two were going out to clubs together at night, with Leah changing out of her thick stockings, long skirt, and tichel into pants and a t-shirt in her friend's apartment.

At first, Leah was intimidated by the idea of going out to clubs. She had been so sheltered all her life and "didn't really know how to talk to a gentile." She was also afraid that her lack of education and experience in the world would be glaringly obvious to everyone she met. After all, what did she know beyond how to make an excellent gefilte fish and *kugel* for fifteen? Would anybody actually be interested in that? In time, however, she began to get more comfortable, and her feelings of inferiority diminished. She started to meet people, even religious people, who were actually accepting—people who treated her with respect and didn't judge her. Little by little, she came to understand that there were other ways to live in the world, and that she had the right to choose a different way.

Surprisingly, Leah's husband didn't seem to care too much about what she was actually doing, although he was always terrified that other people would find out about it and worried obsessively about what might happen if they did. Even so, the two of them sometimes sneaked off together to other parts of the city to go to movies or hang out in bars. He, too, had an outfit to change into: a nice pair of jeans and a baseball cap. Even at their most rebellious, however, neither of them ever ate nonkosher food, and they always observed the Sabbath. And even though they bought a TV, they kept it hidden in the closet and watched it only late at night, so their daughter wouldn't hear or see it.

Over time, the powers that be in Williamsburg started to get wind of what was going on in Leah's life. Leah suspects that someone tapped her phone line, as people in the community began to know things that she talked about only over the phone, mostly with people she had met online. Soon, her friends began receiving calls from people in the community, telling them not to visit Leah's apartment. Leah was also warned by an anonymous caller that she and her husband should stop inviting his divorced male friends over for Shabbos; entertaining so many single men just wasn't appropriate in their community. Leah was outraged. She was the boss in her home and wouldn't dream of telling others what to do in theirs. Besides, whom was she hurting?

But the calls kept coming. And then the letters, threatening Leah with "drastic measures" if she didn't change her ways. She wasn't even sure whom the letters were from or what they were referring to, but she didn't want to stick around to find out. She decided that she had to get out of the community. She could no longer take the feeling of being "choked" all the time. She didn't want to live pretending to be someone she wasn't, pretending to believe in things that she didn't. If she couldn't live her life with some integrity, she preferred not to live at all.

Her husband did not take this very well. It terrified him that his wife was changing, and he was terribly worried about what people would say. He knew perfectly well how embarrassing it would be for him if they divorced, and also that he might never find another wife in the community. But Leah told him that she was moving and taking their child. If he wanted to, he could come with her, but she wasn't going to live in Williamsburg any longer. She just couldn't.

Hoping to work things out, her husband agreed to go along, and they moved to another part of Brooklyn, a more diverse neighborhood with a large population of modern Orthodox Jews and Jamaicans. By that point, however, Leah knew that her marriage was over. She and her husband no longer slept in the same room, and suddenly she couldn't even stand to be in the house with him. When they were home together, she would find herself picking fights with him over little things, like a stain on the rug. Leah began to pressure her husband for a divorce. She knew she had to start becoming her own person. Her husband didn't exactly agree.

After about six months of fighting over whether or not they would get divorced, Leah went to see a rabbi back in Williamsburg. She explained to him that things were so bad that she was going to kill herself if she and her husband were not given permission to separate. And she meant it. The rabbi told her husband to leave the house temporarily. But that turned out to be the end. Leah's husband never came back. He was, of course, extremely hurt, but he left, leaving their daughter, too.

His family, however, was furious, and they decided to put up a fight. They accused Leah of becoming a shiksa, and told her that she had no right to raise her child. If they didn't stop her, she was clearly going to ruin her daughter's life. That is, if she hadn't done so already.

But Leah hadn't come all this way just to let people intimidate her and tell her how to live her life, all over again. She had tried to make things work, staying married for four years, doing her best, putting on the show. And the thought of leaving everything she knew was extremely scary, of course. She had no education and no real understanding of what it meant to hold a full-time job and support a child. But she wasn't going to let fear—or her husband's family—stop her anymore. They had begun spreading gossip about her in the community, trying to convince anyone who would listen that she was unfit to be a mother. At one point, they even offered her money to give up her daughter, so that she could be raised by some of their relatives in a different community. Anything to keep Leah from influencing her own child.

Of course, during their marriage, behind closed doors, Leah and her husband had both been rebellious. They both watched movies and did other forbidden things but, when it came to their divorce, her husband became "the holy one," according to Leah. In fact, in most situations like hers that Leah knew about, the father had ended up with control of the children, even if he didn't end up caring for them himself. But Leah was determined not to let that happen to her.

It was going to be tough, however. Despite her love for her daughter, the pain of Leah's past had begun to catch up with her, and she had finally "exploded." Leah began using drugs, introduced to them by people she had met in clubs and bars. Drugs and alcohol quickly became a way of dulling her pain and escaping the "horrible experiences" of her childhood that seemed to be coming back to haunt her now.

For two years during her separation, Leah used drugs regularly. At one point, she even made the decision to move in with a friend because she was afraid that she could no longer care for her daughter on her own. But Leah knew that if she wanted even a chance of being granted permanent custody of her child, she would have to find a way to stop doing drugs. She got help. She went to AA meetings and, through people she met there, found out about other kinds of groups and seminars as well. Through all of this, she realized that just because her upbringing had been miserable, her life as an adult did not also have to be miserable—she could choose to make it otherwise.

After several false starts and two relapses, Leah managed to give up the drugs and alcohol completely. After two years of fighting in family court (she would never agree to any verdict rendered in a rabbinical court), she also managed to get custody of her daughter. And, to her pleasant surprise, Leah and her husband actually found themselves becoming friends. Now that she had begun to get some help for herself, she had a much easier time relating to her husband. She was able to talk to him openly about things she never could when they were married. They were even able to agree on how they would raise their child.

Today, Leah's daughter is enrolled in a modern Orthodox school. This way, she will get a solid religious education, which Leah thinks is important, but she will also have the opportunity to learn much more as well, as Leah never did. While the school requires that every child's family keep kosher and observe Shabbos, nobody there seems to mind—at least for now—that, as a divorced woman, Leah doesn't cover her hair. Or that, when she comes to pick up her daughter at school, she is usually the only mother wearing pants. Of course, Leah knows that sometimes the whole situation is very confusing for her daughter, who often asks why her mother is no longer Hasidic but her father still is. Leah tries to explain to her that some people are happy being Hasidic, and other people choose to have a different lifestyle, but that every person deserves respect. Someone may dress or look different from you, she tells her daughter, but that is no reason to judge them, and that goes for anyone, religious or not. Her daughter still has questions, and Leah never discourages them, making a point of answering honestly anything she asks.

Leah is not sure that she would be observant at all if she didn't have her daughter at home, even though she still finds herself doing certain things reflexively, like kissing the mezuzah whenever she walks through a doorway that has one, simply out of habit. There was a time when Leah didn't believe in God at all, but that was when she was feeling at her most negative and hopeless. These days, while she doesn't have what she would call a very strong faith, she does feel a kind of spiritual connection to God, a sense that, in the ecumenical language of the Twelve Step programs she attends, there "is a higher power that takes care of me, and has gotten me through all these struggles, and has given me a beautiful child, and made me able to overcome all those things and stand straight." If she ever becomes more religious again, Leah says that it will be because she truly believes, and has a real connection to God—not because she wants to please her neighbors or some larger community.

Still, because Leah has agreed to raise her daughter in an observant home, when they are together she does observe Shabbos and the holidays. She tries her best, however, to make the occasions fun and happy, without pressure or fear. While she might sometimes yell about other things, Leah will never yell at her daughter about anything having to do with religion. Instead, Shabbos and other rituals are carried out "in a loving way," with singing and dancing and lots of hugs. This way Leah makes sure that her daughter is experiencing a joyful, spiritual connection to God, rather than enduring something painful, done for the benefit of other people. And, while there are times when Leah will sneak a cigarette, or listen to the radio in her room with the door closed on Shabbos (both of which are against Jewish law), she still sees the peace and beauty in having a day of rest and isn't about to desecrate it in front of her daughter.

For someone who has been through so much, today Leah seems amazingly free of any bitterness, either about her family or the larger Hasidic community in which she was raised. For a long time, she was envious of people who had grown up in happy homes, and who seemed to believe that being loved and supported was normal and natural—like some of her Hasidic friends, whose mothers offer to baby-sit for their grandchildren so that their daughters can go off for nice evenings with their husbands. Today Leah believes that her experiences have actually made her a stronger person than she ever would have been otherwise. Now she is someone who is not afraid to stand up for herself, and who feels compassion for other people who are suffering or in need of support.

Leah's decision to move out of the community and away from the Hasidic way of life has, understandably, been very hard for her family to accept. But Leah also understands that, for them, much of what one does in life is not merely a matter of personal choice, but of what one has been commanded to do by God. Expecting her parents to accept that she might eat nonkosher food or wear pants, then, is not really fair, or right. Leah knows that she cannot ask her parents to condone behavior that, in their eyes, goes "against their Torah, against their God." Tolerance is, by definition, not one of their virtues.

Not everyone in her family has reacted with disapproval to Leah's decision to leave the Hasidic way of life, however. Of all of her siblings, one brother in particular has been extremely supportive, insisting, against the objections of other family members, that she come to his wedding, and making special visits to her apartment to tell her how much he cares about her, and how wrong her parents were to treat her as they did when they were all growing up. In fact, one afternoon her brother actually came over and watched a movie with her, and also revealed then that there were many times when he wanted to cut his peyos and shave his beard, but that he was too afraid to rock the boat. He was worried that he would receive the same treatment she had.

Leah thinks that she is a much more moral person now than she ever was when she was living in the Hasidic community. She no longer feels that she has to lie or hide, or look down on others in order to feel good about herself, as people in the community always looked down on nonreligious Jews and non-Jews. And she doesn't have to judge other people's moral worth by their type of hair covering, or the length of their beard.

Leah knows that her story is used in the community as a cautionary tale. She is constantly hearing from friends still in the community that people assume her life is awful now, and think she must be miserable. This used to make her angry, but now Leah can laugh, because she knows how untrue it is.

Leah also now receives phone calls from men who are still living in her old community, and who want to get together with her, assuming that because she has left that way of life, she must be "a whore"—or at least a madam, willing to put them in touch with other women who might be interested in sex. Leah finds herself having to explain to these men that changing her style of dress and growing her hair doesn't mean that she has no morals or values. In fact, she explains, her values are clearer and stronger than they ever were, and she has more respect for herself today than she did when she was living in the community.

As insulting as hearing from these men can be, Leah doesn't actually take it personally, or even blame them for thinking the way they do, although she doesn't exactly respect them for it, either. For the most part, she knows that they are merely ignorant, believing unquestioningly what they have learned in the community about women and the outside world. They have been taught that most women who leave the community do so because of a sexual transgression; what else, after all, could drive a woman away from their beautiful way of life? They also believe that once a person is living in the outside world, exposed to the evils of secular society, he or she will become as morally corrupt as most of the goyim. These beliefs tend to reinforce each other, to make such men think that now she is a sex-crazed woman with no morals—the exact opposite of what she was raised to be. Of course, Leah knows that there are many Hasidic men who would never even think of approaching her this way—but the number who have is quite striking.

As for the future, Leah is taking it one day at a time. She is still trying to get used to making it through the day without having to depend on any chemical substances. She has a stable job, and so, for once, money is not the issue that it has been in the past. She and her husband continue to be on good terms, and they talk together often about their lives and their hopes for their daughter. Leah still feels sorry that they both had to be the victims of her lack of stability and readiness for marriage, but, to some degree at least, she also knows that the problem was built into the system.

As far as entering into another relationship is concerned, however, Leah admits to having her "confusions." With her history of abuse, and a lifetime of exposure to the community's inflexible ideas about gender and sexuality, figuring out how to have an intimate relationship remains a challenge. More than anything, however, she just wants to reach a point in her own life where she is strong enough to be ready for a healthy, stable relationship with someone else.

Leah also thinks about getting an education eventually, but she is not sure whether she is ready yet. At times, she feels that she would like to do something to help other people, maybe become a drug or alcohol abuse counselor, helping teenagers from the Hasidic community. Apparently, there are many young people from her old community, and from others as well, who have heard of Leah (the cautionary tale). They seem to know what she's been through and seek her out for advice about how to deal with their own challenges and concerns. Sometimes, these young people have problems with drugs and are terrified to talk to their parents. Others, mostly young women, are getting into dangerous sexual situations with men, just as she once did, mostly for the attention. Leah even hears from older women, married ones, who are unhappy with their lives but feel trapped and don't know what to do. To them, she isn't a cautionary tale, but a hero.

Leah thinks that, to some extent, all human beings live for other people, and that life for most of us is about gaining and keeping the approval and acceptance of others. Growing up in the Hasidic community, however, magnifies that natural tendency, almost to the point, Leah believes, that people become more concerned with what others think than even with what *God* thinks—maybe because it's easier to know that other people actually exist. This is the kind of mentality, she thinks, that allows so many in the younger generation to be able to "fake it," wearing shtreimels on Shabbos, for example, but renting movies and listening to hip hop in the car during the rest of the week. And it's also the reason that she had to miss her own cousin's wedding: some of her relatives worried that her skirt wouldn't be long enough, and that such a transgression would embarrass the family.

Despite all of this, Leah still makes an effort with her family. She tries to visit them fairly regularly and, when she goes to her parents' house, she covers her hair and dresses appropriately, out of respect. But it's still not a comfortable environment for her, and being there can be draining. Leah thinks that her parents may make more of an effort to be close if she does, mainly because they have now come to understand the mistakes they made. They seem to see that many of the things they did when she was a child were terribly wrong. And, for her part, Leah has gained a better understanding of how they could possibly have behaved as they did toward her, although she doesn't excuse them. Neither of her parents came from a loving family, and neither had any idea how to express affection. To this day, Leah's mother seems uncomfortable whenever Leah leans in to give her a hug.

Still, Leah has the sense that, deep down, her mother might actually respect or even envy her for having had the courage to stand up for herself and leave a life she didn't feel was right for her. This may be something her mother had wanted to do herself, but was always too fearful and embarrassed to attempt. Not too long ago, Leah's mother told her that before her own marriage she was planning to wear a different kind of hair covering than her family wanted her to. She had picked it out and was looking forward to putting it on after they shaved her head, after the wedding. But on the day before she was to be married, her family took the head covering away from her. They didn't approve of her choice. "She actually wanted to be a little different, and they didn't allow it," Leah tells me. "This goes very deep."

Chapter Eleven

L'Chaim

It was a good six weeks before Yossi stopped joking about how Malkie and I had had him "locked up," although it was clear that he didn't think the whole episode was very funny. In fact, for the first few weeks after his aborted stint in the hospital, Yossi was largely incommunicado, though, as it turned out, this had less to do with any hard feelings on his part than with the fact that he was still as anxious and obsessive as he had been before he went in. Having been removed from the hospital by his family prematurely—to ensure that his father wouldn't come home to find him there—he hadn't actually received much psychiatric care. As a result, Yossi could still barely concentrate enough to dial a phone number, let alone carry on a conversation with anyone.

His grandmother did manage to get him to a doctor soon after they pulled him out of the hospital, however. An anonymous donor from the community had somewhat mysteriously offered, through an intermediary, to foot the bill for his treatment, as long as Yossi agreed to visit a specific psychiatrist, chosen by the donor. Arrangements were made, and every week a Hasidic man came by the house with a check made out to the doctor, and cash for Yossi's carfare to his office. The doctor ended up prescribing some pills, and also recommending that Yossi see a therapist, a modern Orthodox man with a practice in another section of Brooklyn. This, too, was to be paid for by the anonymous donor. Yossi agreed to see the therapist, although after about six weeks, he decided he didn't think it was helping him very much. The therapist was religious and, while he seemed genuinely compassionate, Yossi knew that the therapy would end up revolving around his rejection of religion, and efforts to make him change his mind. He had been through this kind of thing before, during his marriage, and he wasn't going to subject himself to it again. He knew he had problems, but he also knew that they were not going to be solved by praying more, or finding a wife. So Yossi stopped making the appointments, ripped up the checks when they arrived, and pocketed the carfare for himself. After a few weeks like this, the donor heard from the doctor that Yossi had stopped scheduling therapy sessions, and that was the end of the checks and the carfare.

Around the same time, the medication started to kick in. Yossi began to feel a little less anxious, and by early fall, he was more or less back to himself. He still didn't have a job, but he did decide to sign up for Malkie's free GED class. He would prepare for the test and, when he had passed it, apply to college. At least, that was the plan.

Yossi began attending the GED sessions, along with about ten other people, all of whom were also from religious communities and had received almost no secular education. Each of the students was given a book and paired up with a volunteer tutor. Yossi was thrilled with his tutor, Aisha, an attractive, female, African American college student. He figured that working with her would motivate him to come to the weekly sessions, and for a while it did. But then Yossi met a woman and, suddenly, studying for the GED exam started to seem much less appealing and important than it had. He started skipping a few sessions here and there, and slacking off on his homework. Ironically, however, it was the GED class itself that had been responsible for this positive turn in Yossi's romantic life, and thus for taking his attention away from preparing for the GED.

A few weeks before the GED class was to begin, Yossi met a divorced man from his community who, it turned out, was a little like him. He was open-minded and interested in the outside world, and looking for opportunities to explore it. But he didn't know much English, which was frustrating his attempts, and he wanted to learn the language better. Yossi mentioned that he was going to be taking a GED class, and his new friend got very excited. He wanted to know how he, too, could join the class and said that he would do anything for Yossi if he would secure him a place in it. In fact, he could even set him up with a woman, a baal teshuvah he had dated a few times, who would probably be very happy to go out with Yossi. She was looking for a husband, and so far she hadn't come across anyone suitable; most of the men who were born into religious communities (Yossi's friend apparently being an exception) wouldn't even agree to go out with her once, and all of the newly religious men she met seemed too zealous for her taste. Yossi's friend didn't feel that the woman was right for him, so he was willing to make what he thought was a very fair deal: he would introduce Yossi to the woman, and, in return, Yossi would get him into the GED class.

Yossi never bothered to tell him that Malkie's number was available on her organization's Web site (he didn't even mention that she had a Web site), and that all he had to do was call her up himself. He didn't let on that it wasn't necessary to have special clout or connections to gain entry to the class—just a phone and the desire. And he saw no reason to mention that he was no more looking for a religious wife than he was looking to have a sex change operation. The man was desperate, and Yossi liked feeling important, like someone with friends "on the outside." He also really liked the idea of dating a girl. They made the deal.

Yossi met the woman a few days later, and they began going out to fluorescently lit kosher fast-food places in Flatbush and bars and clubs around Times Square. Truthfully, he didn't find her all that attractive, and they didn't have much in common, either. She had grown up in a secular family in New Jersey and had recently decided to explore her Jewish roots, becoming religious and changing her name from Jessica to Zahava. Not having grown up religious, she had certainly had much more experience than the unmarried girls from Yossi's community. She even had a few tattoos, which her new, modest wardrobe mostly covered (the one on her wrist remained a problem). Also, unlike the girls from Yossi's community, she wasn't *shomer negiah*, meaning that she didn't refrain from physical contact during dating. This meant that Jessica/Zahava would hold Yossi's hand when they went out and, after she had a little to drink, kiss him. On some nights, depending on her mood, she would even invite Yossi back to her small apartment, where she was willing to do *almost* anything with him—now that she was religious, there were some limits—although she always made sure to cover all of the religious books on her bedroom bookshelves with towels, so they wouldn't have to witness the profanity of these encounters. Someone she had studied with when she was becoming religious had told her this was necessary. Yossi found it hilarious.

This relationship with Zahava was a welcome development in Yossi's life. Except for his wife, she was the only woman he had ever been with whom he didn't have to pay for sex, although he did end up spending a lot of money buying her drinks at the bars they went out to together. And even though they really didn't have much to talk about, talking wasn't what Yossi was most interested in. Within about a month, however, Yossi noticed that he was beginning to get a little bored with Zahava, and also fed up with having to find ways to get enough money to take her out. He found he was more interested in watching her cable TV than even in having sex; he had become a big fan of *Curb Your Enthusiasm* on HBO.

For her part, Zahava began to question the seriousness of Yossi's religious commitment, noticing that he didn't seem particularly strict about eating kosher food, or wearing tzitzit, or even waiting until the end of Shabbos to ride the train. He had begun to let his hair grow a little longer and to trim his beard so it wasn't as scraggly, and Zahava did think he looked nice. She also liked the fact that he was open-minded, but she certainly hadn't made such a drastic change in her life and joined the religious community only to become involved with someone who seemed to be moving in the other direction. Their relationship began to cool. But, for the first time, Yossi felt that maybe he was someone girls could like and want to spend time with.

Emboldened by his experience with Zahava, Yossi began to approach girls in bars with more confidence, although not before he had had at least one Long Island Iced Tea. In fact, sometimes Yossi didn't even have to do the approaching. With his more neatly trimmed beard, thick dark hair, and casual wardrobe—by this time, Stan had given him more hand-me-downs, including some old Ralph Lauren sweaters and shirts—Yossi had actually become a cute guy. He even seemed to carry himself a little differently in Stan's clothes than he did in his Hasidic garb, in which he usually hunched his shoulders and walked stooped over, "like an alter kakher." Men in the community were taught to keep their heads down, or their gazes trained on the horizon, to avoid possible eye contact with a woman.

Yossi's grandmother generally turned a blind eye to his escapades. She even packed him lunches—usually a lox sandwich and two bottles of beer—to take with him into the city. But she still remained hopeful that he would find some kind of job. She was all for his studying for the GED and applying to college, as she understood how important it was to have a degree if one wanted to make a good living. Yossi's father knew nothing of Yossi's college plans, but that was OK with Yossi because it only would have encouraged him to call Yossi on his cell phone and scream and yell. Yossi was beginning to feel more and more grateful for his grandmother. In fact, he had no idea what he would do without her.

Even though Yossi occasionally stopped by his parents' apartment to pick up something that belonged to him, or to see his sister or his other siblings, he and his father were still not getting along any better than they had been. If his father was at home when Yossi stopped by, the visits often ended with his father telling him he was worthless. Sometimes he would then chase after him with an electric razor, trying to get Yossi to let him cut the hair on the top of his head short, so that the pieces on the side would look longer, like peyos. There were times when Yossi gave in to the pressure and let him do it. At other times, he managed to get away unscathed. His father still didn't know that Yossi no longer kept kosher or observed the Sabbath, that he didn't do much of anything religious and was out late at night in bars, with girls. He still seemed to believe that Yossi's "rebellion" was mostly about wanting to have a more modern "look." With his father coming at him so often with a razor, Yossi was glad he didn't know the truth.

On one of these visits home, Yossi noticed a book on his parents' kitchen table, written by a doctor with a Jewish-sounding last name. It was about how to understand and deal with "your rebellious child." Yossi flipped through the book and saw that it seemed to have been written for a religious reader, but that it still had some good insights and advice about how to be more loving and accepting toward your children. Around the same time, Yossi's mother started to call him at his grandmother's house, asking him how he was and whether he might want to go for a walk with her. Yossi and his mother had never done this kind of thing before—she had never had the time for it—and he saw that his mother was trying to make an effort. She even told him a few times that she loved him, and gave him cards with sweet sayings in them. But when it became clear that he wasn't going to grow his beard back, that he had no intention of starting up again with "the whole *megillah*," both the phone calls and the walks abruptly stopped.

As fall turned into winter and the days grew shorter and cold, Yossi became more and more antsy, looking for things to do to keep him out of the house and the neighborhood. He was having fun meeting girls, but it wasn't enough to keep his mind going. One day in the middle of December when he was on the subway, he noticed an ad in the *New York Post* for ten-dollar bus rides from New York to Boston. It was a limited-time-only offer that would be expiring in a few days. So right then, Yossi decided to get off the train at Forty-second Street and walk himself over to Port Authority. He didn't know exactly where Boston was, or how long it would take to get there, but for only ten dollars, it seemed like a good way to kill some time. In fact, he had about a hundred dollars in his pocket from a sale he had made earlier that morning to a man in his community—a rare book that he had picked up for twenty dollars at a flea market. It was a tidy, quick profit. But he certainly wasn't one for letting money burn a hole in his pocket.

Yossi was a bit alarmed to learn that the trip to Boston would take over four hours. But the bus was already on the road when he made the discovery, so he decided to sit back and enjoy the ride. He tried to talk to the woman sitting next to him, but she seemed to speak mostly Spanish, so he had to settle for the company of his own thoughts and the views of the bleak winter landscape. The bus was scheduled to arrive in Boston at about 7:30. Yossi figured that when he got there he would go find a bar and get a drink and hang out, maybe meet some interesting people and see the city. He had heard they had some good museums in Boston. He also wanted to check out Brandeis, which he knew was somewhere in the area and had a pretty extensive Yiddish film collection. He thought he would try to see Harvard as well.

What Yossi hadn't bothered to find out before he left New York, however, was that Boston is not an all-night city like New York. Restaurants and bars close around 1:00 a.m., as does the public transportation. He also didn't know that Brandeis is not actually in Boston, but nine miles west of the city, accessible to him only by commuter rail—or, he later learned, the "fuck truck" from Harvard, named for the supposed sexual libertinism of the Brandeis students. The other thing Yossi hadn't realized was that, unlike so many communities in Brooklyn, blue-blooded Boston isn't exactly filled with shtieblech where one could simply knock on someone's door and have a bed, or at least a bench, to sleep on for the night.

When Yossi arrived at South Station in Boston, he had no idea where to go or what to do with himself. He wandered aimlessly around the station for a while, before finally ending up at a pay phone. He was sure that Boston had to have a Chabad House. The Lubavitchers were everywhere, even in Thailand; certainly they would have a place in Boston, particularly with all the schools and young people, so many potential recruits. The rabbi at Chabad would likely take him in for the night, as they had a policy of opening their doors to any and all Jews. From the operator, Yossi got a number and address for the Boston Chabad house, and then began stopping people in the bus station to ask directions to it. After several convoluted explanations from a variety of commuters, he managed to figure out that to get to Chabad, he needed to take something called the Green Line. Yossi was startled to see that Boston had its own kind of subway tokens, and bought an extra one to keep as a souvenir, like currency from a foreign country.

By the time Yossi arrived at the Boston Chabad House, it was close to nine o'clock. He found the rabbi and explained that he was up from New York and needed a place to stay for the night. The rabbi pointed him to a room that apparently belonged to someone who, fortunately for Yossi, was out of town for a few days. Yossi wasn't sure whether to tell the rabbi that he was a Hasid from Brooklyn. He wasn't wearing his garb, and he thought it would probably be best not to get into it. After all, most people who came to Chabad were interested in becoming *more* religious, not giving up religion altogether. Mainly, he was just grateful for the warm room and the bed, particularly because Boston, Yossi had also discovered, was a lot colder than New York.

Yossi spent a few hours out in a bar near the Chabad House, which was close to the campus of Boston University. The city was very different from New York. The streets and buildings looked different, the people sounded different, even the bars felt different, less heimish. He wasn't sure whether he liked Boston or not, but he knew this was probably because he hadn't seen much more of it than the bus station, bar, and Chabad House, and also because it was cold and dark out. But there was one good thing about this city, he noticed:

the drinks were a little cheaper than they were in New York. After two Long Island Iced Teas, Yossi took himself back to the Chabad House and went to bed. He slept in his clothes. By 7:00 a.m. he was up and gone.

Yossi found his way to Cambridge and spent an hour or so walking around Harvard Square. The store windows were all done up with festive Christmas decorations, and there were lights strung through the trees. It was still early, so nothing much was open, except for a few coffee places and a Dunkin Donuts. Yossi went in and bought himself a juice, and he sat there drinking it while flipping through a free local paper full of classified ads. Soon, students began streaming into the place for their bagels and coffee. Most of them were loaded down with heavy book bags. It was hard to tell, from just looking at them, that they were so smart. Harvard students were supposed to be the best, but to Yossi they looked the same as anyone else their age. Still, in a way he envied them. He didn't want to be schlepping around a big heavy bag filled with assignments, but it might have been nice to have the chance.

Yossi finished his juice and decided to check out the campus a little. He saw the library and walked around the outside of some of the dorms in the Yard. He even spent some of his money to go into the Fogg and Busch-Reisinger museums and look around, though he didn't really know what he was looking at. By about 11:30 he didn't know what else to do with himself. And it was bitter cold. So Yossi made his way back to the subway station and got on the train going in the direction of the bus depot. He arrived back in New York at five o'clock, only a little more than twenty-four hours after he had left.

The next week was the final GED class until after the New Year, and even though Yossi hadn't been putting much effort into his studying, and had missed some of the sessions, he definitely wanted to be at the last class. He wanted to thank Aisha and say good-bye to her. He knew she was probably disappointed in him because he had dropped the ball, blowing off his homework and coming in ill-prepared for their meetings. But with Zahava, and going out so much at night, it was hard to keep his focus on algebra problems and photosynthesis. He wondered what knowing about all of that could do for him in life anyway. Maybe he would try to become a stand-up comic. While some people looked at his life and saw tragedy, he liked to say, he preferred to see comedy. Except, of course, when he found himself crying uncontrollably in the bathroom of a seedy bar.

The morning of the day of the last GED class was chilly and damp, and Yossi woke up feeling pretty low. He knew he would have to do something to cheer himself up before heading into the city in the evening for the class. But he also knew that if he had a drink—his current preferred method of generating cheer—Malkie would surely notice and get very angry with him. After all, Yossi knew it wasn't really appropriate to come to class drunk. But he had to do something.

So, sometime around two o'clock, Yossi left his grandmother's house, dressed in his black pants and white shirt, with one of Stan's Ralph Lauren sweaters, a black winter jacket, his kippah, and a black-and-white scarf his grandmother had given him. He put a pair of Stan's jeans in a black plastic bag to take with him, too. When Yossi got to the F train, instead of heading up the stairs to the platform, he turned onto MacDonald Avenue and started walking. He walked for one block, and then one more, and then another, past the bodegas and a shoeshine place, until he arrived at a little barbershop. He went inside and asked one of the barbers how much they charged for a shave. The man told him four dollars. Yossi sat down in the chair and the barber put a towel around his neck.

When Yossi was finished at the barbershop, he still had some time to kill before the GED class. He called me on my cell phone and asked if there was any way I could meet him in about half an hour at the Barnes and Noble in Union Square; he had something he wanted to show me. As it happened, I wasn't far from that neighborhood when he called. I agreed to meet him.

I didn't have my glasses that day, so I couldn't be sure that the figure approaching from the east was Yossi. The man was Yossi's height, had dark hair and the same loose gait, but something was different. He seemed to be standing much taller, less hunched, his head pointed straight ahead rather than down at the sidewalk. And he was taking his time. He kept stopping next to parked cars. It wasn't until he was about ten feet away from me that I knew for sure it was Yossi.

"Hey, Hella! How are ya?" he shouted, his arms in the air. The black plastic bag with the pair of jeans inside dangled from his left arm. "How do I look?" He was still the same Yossi. But he looked like a kid. Shaving the beard had shaved years off his face and his demeanor. For the first time since I'd met him, he actually looked like a man of twenty-five.

Yossi wanted to celebrate and offered to buy me a drink. I told him it was too early for me, but that I would be happy to have a soda. So, we walked a few blocks and found a dark Irish pub. The place was empty, except for one young guy eating chicken pot pie alone in a booth. Yossi wanted to order a beer, but he only had five dollars with him and worried that spending four on a drink would be cutting it a little close. He tried to bargain with the bartender a bit. Though he seemed a bit perplexed at first, the white-haired old Irish guy ultimately took Yossi's *hondling* pretty well, telling him that "four dollars is the price of a beer, old man." I told Yossi I would buy the beer for him. "Thanks a lot," he replied. "L'chaim." To life.

I walked Yossi to his GED class. We arrived there a little early, but one of the other students—a younger man who had left Satmar a year earlier and was hoping to apply to a community college—was already there, sitting and eating a sandwich. When Yossi entered the room, at first the other student didn't recognize him. After about thirty seconds, however, his face lit up with a big smile. He held out his hand and offered Yossi his congratulations, slapping him on the back. As the other students began to trickle in, each one did a double take. They all told Yossi that he looked great, even the ones who still had their beards and were intending to keep them. Everybody asked him whether things would be OK at home, with his father, now that he had made this move. He shrugged and said he didn't know. Even Aisha told him he looked cute.

As everyone congratulated Yossi on the shave, and commented on how good he looked, I couldn't help feeling a tinge of sadness, even through all of the excitement. It was wonderful to see Yossi so happy, so free of worry and anxiety, if only for those few minutes. And he really did look good. But, in a way, I also felt a strange sense of loss. Not for the "old" Yossi, or for the life he had in spirit abandoned even before I had met him, but maybe for all of the things I believed he might now be forced to leave behind. Without his beard, he would probably not be welcomed in shul again, or invited to important celebrations among friends and family. He probably would be too uncomfortable to go to the men's mikvah, which he loved doing because it was so relaxing to sit in the steam and schmooze. Even walking in his neighborhood would be stressful now, with people staring and whispering, and some inevitably insisting on nasty confrontations.

I had come to know Yossi very well by now, and saw many times how his eyes would light up when he told stories about the Hasidim, not only those who had lived in centuries past, but even some he knew today. Like the man who would become ecstatic eating matzoh on Passover, tasting in that dry cracker the freedom of his people, and letting the feeling of gratitude run through his body like an electric current. I had listened to him quote with great fervor Hasidic sages, particularly the one who spoke of learning about love from two drunken paupers in a bar. I had heard him excitedly explain the concept of the *Shekinah,* which is at the heart of the Sabbath and is used to identify God's nearness to man. It is also a concept that, in Kabbalah, represents the feminine aspect of God's presence.

I knew that getting rid of his beard had both practical and symbolic meaning for Yossi. It represented the shedding of a life of myriad restrictions and, with that, the shedding of so much pain as well. But with the beard or without it, Yossi was in fact, as he had tried to explain to his sister that summer after the first shave, the same man underneath. It was difficult to know that he might no longer be accepted as that man by some of the people who should have loved him most in the world. I was certainly thrilled for Yossi, but I was nervous for him as well. Probably just the right combination for a Jewish mother.

This time, Yossi promised himself that he wasn't going to let the beard grow back, no matter what anybody said or did to him. So, after the GED session ended that evening, he grilled the ex-Satmar student about shaving: what brand of razor to buy, how often to use it, how to hold it. Right there in the classroom, he gave Yossi a mock demonstration, explaining how he should wet his face before applying the shaving cream, and how to stretch his skin a little and then angle the razor in the direction the hair grows, making sure to take special care around the creases near his mouth. He also told him about aftershave and what to do about ingrown hairs. Yossi watched and listened with rapt attention, more than he had given to any of the GED material. When he left the classroom that night, he ran right to the nearest drugstore to buy himself shaving supplies.

So far, Yossi has kept his promise to himself. These days he remains clean-shaven, which is less of a testament to his technical skill with a razor than to his resolve under pressure. The second shave actually didn't cause as much of a stir as the first one, although when Yossi's father heard about it, not surprisingly, he became very angry and upset all over again. In fact, he told Yossi that, for all he cared, Yossi "could go live out in the snow," that he was not welcome in his house ever again, even to visit, and that this impulsive act was going to ruin any chance of a good shidduch for his sister, who had just started to look for a husband.

More recently, Yossi's father has calmed down a bit, mainly because Yossi's sister is now engaged to a boy, and everyone seems to think that it's a very good match. This turn of events has certainly raised his father's mood, and has also taken some of the pressure off Yossi, at least for now. There is no way he can be blamed for destroying his sister's future, at least not yet. His sister's engagement has also made Yossi genuinely happy, mainly because his sister is so excited about it herself—although it is still hard for him to believe that she would want to marry someone after knowing him for only twenty minutes, and when the whole meeting revolved around where their future kids would go to school and what kind of bekishe the husband would wear on Shabbos (he is apparently a studious type who wants to wear a particular style of bekishe and white knee socks, signifying his status as a scholar). Yossi also worries that her naïveté about sex might make it less pleasurable for her than it should be, but he knows she would recoil in horror were he to impart any advice.

It also seems that everyone in Yossi's family—his father included—wants Yossi to be present at all of the simchas, or engagement parties, and, of course, at the wedding itself, to share in the family's joy. But his father has already made it very clear to him that if Yossi wants to attend any of these celebrations, he must have a beard on his face, lest the groom see him clean-shaven and then decide to back out before the marriage has actually taken place. So far, it appears that the boy and his family don't know anything about Yossi, probably because they are not from the same community. While Yossi is holding out some hope that by the time the wedding rolls around, his family might be OK with having him there without a beard, he knows in his heart that this won't be the case. But he also doesn't think it would be fair to his sister not to come—what would he do, pretend to be on a very long, around-the-world vacation, and wish his new brother-in-law congratulations by phone? Right now, he is considering growing back his beard temporarily, just for the wedding day, "like a Hollywood actor who changes his look for a part," because he knows that his being there will make his sister very happy.

Of course, Yossi also knows that even in the unlikely event that his father ever stops bothering him about the beard, he will still never truly accept him for who he is. His father knows almost nothing about his life, about what he really thinks and feels about so many things—not just religious issues, but about life and people and the world in general. In fact, a few weeks ago, Yossi's father came across something Yossi had written many years ago for school, in response to a passage of Talmud. He called Yossi on his cell phone to tell him how brilliant it was, and how reading it made him believe that someday Yossi would actually return to the fold. Apparently, there is a saying, which his father quoted to him, that among those who go off the path, it is the ones who are the most learned who have the best chance of coming back. Unlike the lazy ones, or the merely rebellious, or the stupid, those who are real scholars have the necessary foundation. Because Yossi would rather not burst his father's bubble and bring any more problems on himself, for now, at least, it's fine with him to let his father hope.

It also turns out that—hard as it is for him to believe—Yossi doesn't have much trouble meeting girls anymore. In fact, now they are chasing after him. Of course, it hasn't hurt that Yossi doesn't always tell women the whole truth about himself, fearing that most wouldn't want to date someone who hasn't been to college, who works only sporadically, and who, at twenty-five, still lives with his grandmother. So far, Yossi has made himself into a film director and a producer. One girl even took him out to a big, expensive lunch to pitch him her script. He felt a little guilty about this, and so the director and producer "are now retired." But they still had a good time and a nice meal; it was the first time he had ever eaten oysters.

Yossi would rather not have to make up professions for himself, but so far he continues to have little luck finding work, or finding the motivation to work at the things he is qualified to do. He does have a new tutoring gig—another child of newly religious parents—but the kid really isn't all that interested in learning what Yossi has been hired to teach him, and Yossi can't help identifying with the kid's resistance. He also feels like more and more of a hypocrite each day, trying to make the boy learn things that he himself doesn't believe in. The money is pretty good, but Yossi doesn't know how long his conscience will continue to let him do it. He also still thinks about going to college, but he hasn't taken the GED yet, and he is not sure he feels prepared enough to try. Maybe he will try to buy a transcript from his old yeshiva, after all. That is, if he can steel himself to go in there and withstand the scrutiny, without his beard.

Lately, Yossi has been running into a lot of young men like himself, in what he once would have thought were pretty unlikely places, like bars in big converted warehouses in non-Hasidic Williamsburg, the corners of Socialist used book stores, or the aisles of Barnes and Noble stores. Of course, it is easy for him to spot the ones who are dressed in Hasidic garb. Even those who are wearing jeans and baseball caps tend to give themselves away, however, with their long beards and body language and telltale Yiddish accents. Yossi gets a kick out of approaching these men—who often try to avoid making eye contact with him at first—and talking to them in Yiddish, introducing himself and explaining that he understands what they might be going through. Some of them aren't interested in talking to him and just walk away. But others are grateful that he has noticed them, and that he made the effort to connect. He always tells these people he meets that he is not looking to convert anyone, or influence them in any way, but that he is just open to hanging out, to being friends. He tells them that he knows what it's like to be rejected, and to have to sneak around and lie a lot. And he knows from experience that sometimes it's better if you don't have to do it all alone.

In fact, Yossi has been thinking a lot about starting his own movement, a kind of neo-Hasidic society, where Hasidim—men *and* women—who feel as he does, and anyone else who wants to, could come to participate in and enjoy the "great" things about Hasidic culture, without the pressure and the judgment, the need for hiding and secrecy. His movement would celebrate the music, the wild dancing and singing, the mystical philosophy, the Eastern European and also Sephardic food, the tales and stories, perhaps even some of the funkier garb, like the shtreimels and the bekishes, and maybe even the women's wigs, for those who are into dressing up. He would find a space and fix it up, make it stylish and swank, with comfortable seating, nice lights, and a big, well-stocked bar. And he would build a dance floor where men and women could dance together, and maybe there would even be space somewhere for kids. And everyone else would be welcome, too: other types of Jews, Gentiles—blacks, whites, browns, gays, straights, questionings, you name it. It wouldn't be about trying to convince anyone to remain religious, or to become religious, or even to reject religion. In fact, it wouldn't be about convincing anyone of anything at all. It would just be about being with people and celebrating the good things in life, the happy things that make everyone feel that they belong and have a place. Indeed, to Yossi, this would be the realization of his own American dream.

Conclusion

Like anyone who undertakes intensive field research, I had no idea where that first dinner at Suri's house might lead me, and what I would learn from the journey—about the people I would meet, about the communities they lived in or had left, and, of course, about myself. Nor did I have any idea what larger meanings might emerge from this experience, or how what I saw and participated in "on the ground" might fit into or reflect some broader context.

In some ways, my lack of prior involvement with Hasidic life and observant Judaism in general made this project quite daunting. Not only was gaining access a significant issue, at least initially, but so also was the learning curve, which was quite steep. Indeed, throughout the research process, I spent many hours reading and asking people about different aspects of Jewish law, ritual practice, and custom that I, at times, felt somewhat ashamed not to be familiar with—after all, even if it had been left somewhere very far behind, this was undeniably my heritage, too. But my lack of personal involvement with religious life also meant that I came to this subject without the often intense emotional commitments and passionately held points of view that inhere in those for whom religious observance and affiliation are matters of great importance. Having had so little prior exposure to this world also made me notice and question certain beliefs, attitudes, and practices that, had I possessed more knowledge or experience going in, I might have taken for granted.

This is not to claim, however, that I didn't have my own reactions to what I saw and heard. Of course I did, and they seemed to grow more layered and complex as time went on. When I first began visiting Hasidic communities, even casually, the differences between Hasidic life and my own were so glaring that they could easily have obscured the obvious fact that Hasidic people are, of course, *people*. While distinctive for their commitment to living as members of tightly knit ideological and behavioral communities apart from the mainstream, they are also individuals, who have thoughts and feelings and dreams and desires, just like everybody else. In fact, it was my early encounter with Suri and Chanie that first illuminated this truth for me so clearly.

My time spent in Hasidic communities opened up entire new worlds to me. I learned something about the various permutations of Hasidic philosophy—though by no means in the depth required to claim real understanding—and also about Hasidic ritual practice. I saw and experienced what went on at home, in the everyday lives of some Hasidic families, as well as how daily life played out in the more public spaces of Hasidic communities. Some aspects of this way of life seemed rather exotic, and others almost startlingly familiar, and there were certainly things that I learned and experienced that struck me as both beautiful and compelling. But, because my research developed in the way that it did, I also became aware of things about this world that were quite troubling—things that I didn't want to see as connected to Judaism or Jewish people in any way.

For the most part, this reaction had little to do with what I learned about Jewish law itself, or even Hasidic belief and custom, although there is certainly much in both that would be difficult for me to embrace personally. However, as a way of living in the world, of giving meaning to and deriving meaning from human activity, there is also much to admire as well: Hasidism's powerful insights into human psychology, its deep wisdom about social life, and the opportunities it grants for a spiritual connection to something beyond oneself—that is, to God.

Some of the discomfort for me, however, came in seeing just how far life in Hasidic communities can fall short of Hasidism's ideals. Of course, this gap between the ideal and what is practiced is not unique to Hasidism, and many people I spoke with liked to claim, as a kind of defense, that it is not the religion itself, but religious people who are the problem. This may be a more intellectual than substantive distinction, however. Religion, of course, does not exist in a vacuum, and even those who believe that religious laws were handed down from God acknowledge that it has been up to human beings to interpret them and carry them out. The lives of those described in this book unfolded within actual Hasidic communities, after all, not in some theoretical space.

For many people today, the erosion of traditional communities and the way of life they foster has become cause for great concern. For some, this concern stems from an ideological commitment to the values and behaviors that have been an intrinsic part of traditional community life. For others, it is a profound sense of nostalgia for their own past, or some imagined and longed-for ideal, that fuels these concerns. To many such people, Hasidic life, at least on its surface, stands as a potent reminder of what has been lost. These are real neighborhoods, communities whose members share a common set of values and practices, and who know and seem to care about one another.

Indeed, there is a growing body of literature documenting the shift from geographical location to identity as a major determinant of group membership. This change has resulted from a combination of factors, including the growth of "identity politics," as well as advances in technology that have allowed individuals with similar concerns and orientations to connect with each other even across great geographical distances. These days, it is not hard to find people who feel they have almost nothing in common with their neighbors, and often do not even know what they look like.

In the end, however, the Hasidim are not a community defined exclusively by the fact that they live much of their lives within certain physical borders. On the contrary, they form a primarily ideological community, which, despite a premodern worldview, is bound together by a very postmodern concern with identity. The Hasidic identity, however, is not one that is determined or defined solely by religious belief or even practice, but also by a sense—both real and imagined—of a shared history and potential future fate.

One of the most striking things I came to understand during the course of this research is the power of the Holocaust, and the history of Jewish suffering in general, both in the actual lives of some Hasidic people and in the imaginations of these communities as a whole. There is, of course, the plain historical fact that the Hasidic communities that exist in America today were started almost entirely by refugees from World War II. It would be hard to overstate how deeply affected by their wartime experiences these people were, how receptive those who had, in many cases, lost everything must have been to the sense of solace, dignity, and hope these communities provided. Indeed, even today, while most Hasidic people learn a very limited amount of post-Biblical history—one man I interviewed told me that his grandmother was born in "Germany, Hungary, or Europe, it really doesn't matter"—they all know the name of Adolf Hitler.

With its history of religious tolerance and commitment to pluralism, America was an ideal place for these refugees to set about recreating their way of life. However, as it has turned out, the very same American values that allowed these communities to flourish also enabled them to become increasingly closed and insular, shutting themselves off from the larger world and its concerns, living in fear of bringing about another Holocaust through assimilation and the abandonment of a "Torah life." Ironically, what began as a poignant and heroic effort in the face of utter devastation and loss has led, generations later, to communities in which nonconformity can subject members to the kinds of stigmatization and ostracism that have, throughout history, characterized the treatment of Jews by the outside world.

Apprehending this sad irony was one of the most upsetting consequences of my involvement with this research. Work done in psychology tells us that it is not unusual for those who have been victimized to become victimizers themselves—"identification with the oppressor," it is sometimes called. However, even ignoring their particular history, the intolerance of these communities would still be striking; in a country that holds individual freedom and expression among its highest stated ideals, those who emphasize other values can seem both alien and threatening.

But ultimately, it was not this focus on the primacy of the group over the individual that was troubling to me, but rather the extent to which fear seemed to regulate behavior and maintain conformity in these communities, ultimately reproducing their way of life, one generation after the next. In some cases, it was the fear of God's wrath, or of ending up in hell—something not limited, of course, to Orthodox Jewish theology—that drove people to conform, even against their will. In many others, it was the fear of the community that motivated behavior. In fact, there were several people who agreed to participate in this research, only to call me at some later point—sometimes in the middle of the night—to express their concerns about their participation.

While some of these people were still living in their communities, others had already left them behind. In most cases, their concerns were related to the terrible fear of exposure, and of retribution through the shaming of family members and close relatives. In a few cases, however, people explained to me that they had come to worry that to express openly their negative feelings actually represented what is known as a *Chilul Hashem*, or a desecration of God's name. Interestingly, those who raised this latter concern were always women, and, in every case, they had reached this conclusion at the urging of their husbands. That there exists a religious concept that supports and reinforces people's fear of voicing dissenting views, expressing discontent, or even revealing that they were the victims of abuse makes it easier to understand why so many people are driven into lives of secrecy and hiding, of putting towels over the windows, changing their clothes on the subway, and keeping their mouths shut.

In no way do I mean to suggest that a belief in the Hasidic worldview and the social, emotional, and spiritual rewards of living as a Hasidic Jew do not also play an important role in maintaining and perpetuating these communities. But even those who identified themselves as contented members of their communities nonetheless expressed a great preoccupation with what others in the community would think, and say, and do in the face of even hypothetical nonconformity. Notably, however, many such people liked to point out to me that everyone everywhere lives in some kind of community, and that the pressure to conform, as well as the fear of the ramifications of not doing so, are universal characteristics of social life.

I have spent a lot of time considering this point of view. Understanding the interplay between the individual and the larger social structures of which he or she is a part is one of the most basic concerns of sociology. The degree to which individuals are able to interpret, resist, and reshape the larger social forces that operate on their lives is the subject of great debate within the discipline. However, even putting aside the more profound philosophical questions about the ultimate nature and existence of individual freedom, the suggestion that *everyone* is concerned with—indeed structures his or her life around—other people's opinions and perceptions does little to illuminate the particular situation of the Hasidim.

Why is it that fear and shame played, and in some cases continue to play, such critical roles in the lives of the people I came to know throughout this project? Certainly these communities have a clear interest in suppressing or ridding themselves of those members whose nonconformity undermines community stability. Among people who believe that there is only one truth—and that they are in possession of it—tolerating other points of view is, by definition, impossible. However, while I tried my best to remain open to all points of view, I couldn't help feeling angered by the treatment many had been subjected to, merely for asserting their individual desires, or daring to question. There is no doubt that parents suffer greatly when a child rejects their way of life and everything they believe in.

When their beliefs tell them that, in so doing, their child will suffer, it must be excruciating. At the same time, however, the need to coerce people's behavior through fear and shame suggests a fundamental weakness in the belief system itself. To feel forced to abuse or reject a loved one for his or her failure to conform to community standards seems to negate any claim to true religiousness. But this is the paradox of fundamentalism.

In the end, however, those I met in the course of this research—Malkie and Yitzchak and Dini and Chaim and Leah and, of course, Yossi—demonstrate that, despite just how daunting it can be, people still retain the power to resist and, ultimately, to make a different choice. Or at least right now, in America, they do.

For close to fifty years, scholars have been predicting the demise of these communities, forecasting their inevitable inability to resist the pull of the vast American mainstream. So far, they have been proven wrong, and I wouldn't want to risk joining their company by making any predictions. But, if the lives of those described in this book are any indication, it appears that something might have to change sometime soon. While Yossi's dream of a secular Hasidic society might represent the worst kind of heresy to any observant Jew, the sentiments fueling it reflect the tensions that exist within so many who are forced—given the all-or-nothing attitude toward religion they have been taught—to make a decisive break with their pasts, their families, and even with the Jewish tradition more generally. Perhaps through their unique experiences as "native-born immigrants" possessed of a rich heritage and a hard-won openness to the world beyond its contours, they will pave the way for change, or for something new.

Glossary

Note: the Yiddish transliterations used here and throughout the book do not follow the standard YIVO orthography. Instead, they were developed with the people who appear in this book and reflect their sensibilities.

alter kakher—(literal translation: old shitter) An old fart; a complaining old person

apikoros—Unbeliever; heretic

baal teshuvah/baalei teshuvah (pl.)—(literal translation: master of return) A penitent; a Jew who returns to a traditional observant Jewish lifestyle (also known by the acronym BT)

Baruch Hashem—(literal translation: Blessed is Hashem) Thank God

beis medrash—Jewish house of study

bekishe—A long silk coat worn by men, mostly on the Sabbath, and fastened with a prayer belt called a *gartel*

bris—The Jewish rite of circumcision, performed on a male on his eighth day of life

Chabad—Acronym for chochma, bina, daas (wisdom, understanding, knowledge); a synonym for Lubavitch, the branch of the Hasidic movement founded by Rabbi Schneur Zalman of Liadi

challah—Loaf of yeast-leavened egg bread, usually braided, traditionally eaten by Jews on the Sabbath, holidays, and other ceremonial occasions

chassidus—The teachings of the various Hasidic rebbes; Hasidic philosophy

cholent—Traditional Sabbath dish usually made with meat, potatoes, and beans

chutzpah—Nerve; gall; willingness to flout convention

daven—To pray

frum—Religious; pious

goy/goyim—(literal translation: nation) A non-Jew/non-Jews

Halacha—Talmudic literature that deals with law and with the interpretation of the laws on the Hebrew Scriptures

halachically—According to Jewish law

haredi/haredim—Strictly Orthodox Jews (used primarily in Israel)

Hashem—(literal translation: "the Name") Noun used in place of the word "God"

Haskalah—Jewish Enlightenment movement (1770s–1880s), which began in Germany in the circle of the German Jewish philosopher Moses Mendelssohn and spread to Galicia and Russia. The movement called for civic emancipation of the Jews through secular learning, a concern for aesthetics, and linguistic assimilation (especially in Germany). The proponents of the Haskalah, called Maskilim, established schools and published periodicals and other works. By publishing in Hebrew, they contributed to the revival of the language.

heimish—Homelike; warm; welcoming; folksy

hondel/hondling—To bargain/bargaining

Kabbalah/Kabbalistic—(literal translation: to receive) The mystical interpretation of the Jewish Scriptures. The Kabbalah has two principal written sources: *Sefer Yezira*, a third-century work that purports to present a series of monologues given by the patriarch Abraham, and the *Zohar*, a mystical commentary on the Torah written by Moses de León in the thirteenth century. As a religious movement, it appears to have started in eleventh-century France and then spread to Spain and elsewhere. Kabbalah influenced the development of Hasidism in the eighteenth century.

kippah—(Hebrew) A skullcap; called a *yarmulke* in Yiddish

klutz—A clumsy person

kollel—(Hebrew) Community or group; center for advanced Torah studies

kugel—A baked pudding, made with potatoes or noodles and sometimes meat and vegetables

landsman—Fellow countryman; fellow townsman from the old country

lashon hara—(literal translation: evil tongue) Understood to encompasses all forms of forbidden speech such as gossip, slander, lying, and the like. It is said that lashon hara is worse even than murder, because through it three people are killed: the speaker, the listener, and the one of whom it is spoken.

l'chaim—(literal translation: to life) The traditional Jewish toast

Litvish—Yiddish for Lithuanian Jews; Ashkenazi Jews who have their origins in historic Lithuania

macher—(literal translation: maker) A successful or important person

mazel—Luck

mechitza—Divider used to separate men and women in synagogue and other public places

megillah—Tractate of the Talmud; also, a long, drawn-out story

meshugas—Craziness

mezuzah—Scroll inscribed on one side with Biblical passages and inserted in a small case that is attached to the doorpost of the home

mikvah—Ritual bath used for purification

Misnagdim—(literal translation: opponents of the Hasidim) Non-Hasidic, strictly Orthodox Jews

mitzvah/mitzvot (pl.)—Commandment; act of kindness

moser/mesira—Informer/the act of informing

Moshiach—Messiah

niddah—State of ritual impurity brought on by uterine bleeding

Pesach—Passover

peyos—Side curls. The justification for peyos can be found in Leviticus 19:27, which states that "You shall not round the corners of your heads, nor shall you mar the corners of your beard." Hasidim (and other haredi Jews) interpret this to mean that men should not be clean-shaven or cut off the hair around the temples.

Purim—Holiday celebrated a month before Passover, commemorating the victory of the Jews over Haman, who sought to slay the Jews of ancient Persia. The main ritual of Purim is the recitation in synagogue of the Scroll of Esther, which tells the story of Haman's attack on the Jews. Also, children (and some adults) dress up in costumes, Purim greetings are sent from house to house, accompanied by food, and charity is given to the poor. While Jews are required to give charity all year, there is an additional commandment to give charity on Purim.

rebbe—(literal translation: teacher) Leader of a Hasidic group

Rosh Hashanah—Holiday marking the beginning of the Jewish New Year

schlep—Drag around

schmooze—Chat; an informal conversation

seforim (pl.)—Jewish religious books

Shabbos—The Sabbath

shaitel—A wig

shatnes—Halachically prohibited mixture of linen and wool

shidduch—Match; arranged marriage

shiksa/shaigetz—A derogatory term for a non-Jewish woman/man

shiva—Seven days of mourning after the burial of a close relative

shluchim—Emissaries; outreach workers

shomer negiah—A religious person's abstention from physical contact during dating

shonda—A shame or disgrace; a pity

shpitzel—A head covering that consists of pieces of hair only in the front, the rest covered by a hat or a scarf

shrei/shreiing—Scream/screaming

shtetl—Little town or village. In Europe, before World War II, shtetls were complete communities with their own butchers, bakers, financial institutions, and so forth. They arose partly because Christians forced the Jews into segregated living, and partly because Jews needed to live near a kosher butcher and a shul for practical reasons.

shtick—(literal translation: a piece) A little; a routine; a prank or a piece of clowning; a devious trick

shtiebl/shtieblech (pl.)—(literal translation: a small room) Storefront synagogue

shtreimel—The fur hat that married men from certain (though not all) Hasidic sects traditionally wear on the Sabbath

shtup—(literal translation: to poke, stuff) Fuck; screw

shul—(literal translation: school) Synagogue

simcha(s)—(Hebrew) Celebration(s). Among the Hasidim, this word is usually used to refer to family celebrations.

Simchas Torah—(Hebrew) (literal translation: "celebration of the Torah") A festival celebrating the Law of Moses and the completion of the year's cycle and subsequent new beginning. Observed on the 22nd or 23rd day of the Hebrew month of Tishri.

sofer—Ritual scribe

Taharas Hamishpacha—Laws of family purity

tallis—A four-cornered prayer shawl worn by men during the morning prayers

Talmud—Collection of ancient rabbinic writings on Jewish law and tradition (consisting of the Mishna and the Gemara) that constitute the basis of religious authority in Orthodox Judaism

tefillin—Either of two small leather boxes containing texts from the Hebrew Scriptures, traditionally worn on the forehead and the left arm by Orthodox Jewish men during morning prayer

tichel—Head scarf worn by women

tikkun olam—(literal translation: world repair) The phrase has origins in classic rabbinic literature and Kabbalah. In modern Jewish circles, it has come to mean "repairing the world" through social action in the form of outreach, the pursuit of social justice, and involvement in charity.

tish—Table

Torah—The first five books of the Hebrew Scriptures; a scroll of parchment containing the first five books of the Hebrew Scriptures used in a synagogue during services; the entire body of religious law and learning, including both sacred literature and oral tradition

tuchus—Behind; ass

tzitzit—The fringes of knotted string at the four corners of the prayer shawl, traditionally symbolizing the mitzvot

yeshiva—An institute of learning where students study sacred texts, primarily the Talmud; an elementary or secondary school with a curriculum that includes religion and culture as well as general education

Yeshivish—A word usually used to refer to non-Hasidic, strictly Orthodox Jews, also known as Litvish

yiches—Family status or prestige; good pedigree

Yom Kippur—The day of atonement and the holiest day of the Jewish year

Acknowledgments

This project draws on research done for my Ph.D. in sociology, and I owe thanks to my dissertation chairman, William Helmreich, and to my other committee members, Paul Attewell and Cynthia Fuchs Epstein.

Of course, the very nature of this subject prohibits me from acknowledging those people who contributed the most to this book, by giving of themselves, often despite their fears of exposure. Without their help, writing this book would have been impossible. They know who they are, and I thank them for trusting me to help tell their stories. Malkie Schwartz is one person whose participation I can acknowledge openly, and it is not an exaggeration to say that without the candor, generosity, intelligence, patience, and courage she showed me, and continues to show the world, this book would have been significantly lacking.

I also want to thank my great friend, who just happened to become my agent, Rob McQuilkin, for without him this book might never have made it into print. It is a testament to his professionalism and grace as a human being that our twenty-year friendship not only remained unscathed by, but became even stronger through, this collaboration.

I want to thank Linda Winston for the time she spent listening to me, and for her cogent advice. I also want to thank Paul Winston, for reasons too numerous to list here, and Josefina Vásquez, for her skill with a camera and casual attitude toward uninvited guests. I am grateful to Peter Weitzner for his advice. I also thank Robert Klein for his careful reading of drafts and Sylvia Schönberg for being such a willing and gracious hostess. Stanley Klein also has my gratitude for square rooting it many times, as does Claudia Gutwirth, for being such a careful, close reader and unqualified supporter. I am also grateful to Alan Rinzler for his suggestions as an early reader, and for the enthusiasm he showed for this project.

I am indebted to Rabbi Abraham Unger, who answered my questions patiently, and who supported this work with openness and sensitivity. And Joyce Goodman also has my thanks for listening, discussing, commenting, and laughing, as does Krina Patel, for long hours spent on the phone and in her kitchen. I want to thank Susan Weidman Schneider for her interest in this material, and for publishing an early version of some of it in *Lilith* magazine. And I want to thank Joe Queenan for being so encouraging about this work from the start. I have also received a tremendous amount of support from Justin Richardson.

My editor at Beacon Press, Amy Caldwell, deserves my gratitude for giving me this opportunity, as well as her guidance and support throughout this process. I also want to thank Kathy Daneman and Tom Hallock for their sensitivity and hard work on behalf of this project; Lisa Sacks, for her attention to detail and patience; and Foxxe Editorial Services for the cogent comments and very careful copyedit.

Finally, I would like to thank my father, for always being so open and curious, and for teaching me to be the same. And I want to thank my mother, whose own complicated history no doubt played a significant role in my choosing this subject matter, and whose example as an artist and a human being has allowed me to see how, out of the mess of life, it might be possible to make something like art.

Notes

Introduction

1. See Lis Harris, *Holy Days: The World of a Hasidic Family* (New York: Touchstone, 1995); Sue Fishkoff, *The Rebbe's Army: Inside the World of Chabad Lubavitch* (New York: Schocken, 2003); Stephanie Wellen Levine, *Mystics, Mavericks, and Merrymakers: An Intimate Journey Among Hasidic Girls* (New York: NYU, 2003).

2. Current estimates put the total U.S. Lubavitch population at about thirty thousand. See Fishkoff, *The Rebbe's Army*. According to "Jewish Demography — 5759 (1999), Part II," by M. Samsonowitz, as of 1999, the total U.S. Satmar population was estimated to be close to seventy thousand, with thirty thousand living in Williamsburg, seventeen thousand in Monroe, N.Y., fifteen thousand in Boro Park, and five thousand in Monsey (see http://chareidi.shemayisrael.com/archives5759/ach_ked/AKdemog.htm). Given the high birth rates in the Satmar community, one can assume that the number is higher today.

3. Fishkoff estimates that there are anywhere from eighty thousand to one hundred thousand Lubavitchers living outside the United States. This number is impossible to confirm, however, and is likely to include those who identify with Lubavitch without fully committing to the lifestyle.

4. See Fishkoff, *The Rebbe's Army*.

5. See Wellen Levine, *Mystics, Mavericks, and Merrymakers*, p. 34. Levine does suggest here that this estimate may be a little high.

6. For scholarly studies of this phenomenon, see: Lynn Davidman, *Tradition in a Rootless World: Women Turn to Orthodox Judaism* (Berkeley: University of California Press, 1993); Debra R. Kaufman, *Rachel's Daughters: Newly*

Orthodox Jewish Women (New Jersey: Rutgers University Press, 1991); Bonnie J. Morris, *Lubavitcher Women in America: Identity and Activism in the Postwar Era* (New York: SUNY Press, 1998); and Herbert M. Danzger, *Returning to Tradition: The Contemporary Revival of Orthodox Judaism* (New Haven: Yale University Press, 1989).

7. See Fishkoff, *The Rebbe's Army*, and David Horovitz, "The Rebbe's Army Marches Forward," *Jerusalem Post*, November 19, 2004.

8. Of course, none of these groups is monolithic, and there is, as in every other Hasidic sect, a range of attitudes, behaviors, and beliefs. That said, Satmar is generally regarded, within the Hasidic world, as the most extreme of the Hasidic sects. Satmar's anti-Zionist stance stems from the Satmar rebbe's view that only the Messiah can return the Jews to the land of Israel. The attempt to create a secular state of Israel through political means represented, to him, a violation of God's laws.

9. It would have been extremely unlikely for Suri to offer to introduce me to Hasidic men, as codes of modesty prohibit women and men in the community from freely socializing.

10. There are strictly Orthodox Jews who are not Hasidic, known as "Yeshivish" or "Litvish," the latter name referring to their historical place of origin in Lithuania. Litvish Jews, or Litvaks, are also known as "Misnagdim," or "opponents" of the Hasidim, and historically they have tended to stress religious scholarship over Hasidism's more mystical approach. While these two groups have much in common, the Litvaks tend to emphasize male scholarship even over work, which has not traditionally been the case with the Hasidim, although in recent years this has been changing. For more on this, see William Helmreich, *The World of the Yeshiva: An Intimate Portrait of Orthodox Jewry* (Jersey City, NJ: Ktav, 2000). Still, it is much more common for Litvish women to go to work (to support their husbands' studies) than it is for Hasidic women.

11. See Jerome R. Mintz, *Hasidic People: A Place in the New World* (Cambridge, MA: Harvard University Press, 1992) and Israel Rubin, *Satmar: Two Generations of an Urban Island* (New York: Peter Lang, 1997). A notable exception is Tamar El-Or's *Educated and Ignorant: Ultraorthodox Women and Their World* (Boulder, Colorado, and London: Lynne Rienner Publishers, 1994).

12. www.footstepsorg.org

13. See Janet Belcove-Shalin, ed., *New World Hasidism: Ethnographic Studies of Hasidic Jews in America* (Albany, New York: State University of New York Press, 1995).

Chapter One

1. See Egon Mayer, *From Suburb to Shtetl: The Jews of Boro Park* (Philadelphia: Temple University Press, 1979).

2. Ibid.

3. See Bryan Mark Rigg, *Rescued from the Reich: How One of Hitler's Soldiers Rescued the Lubavitcher Rebbe* (New Haven: Yale University Press, 2004), pp. 171, 182.

4. See *Va'Yoel Moshe,* by Satmar Grand Rebbe Joel Teitelbaum (Jerusalem Bookstore, Inc., 1961, 2004), Section 110.

5. The seventh, and most recent, Lubavitcher rebbe reversed this stance, claiming that we cannot know the reasons for the Holocaust.

6. See Jerome R. Mintz, *Hasidic People: A Place in the New World* (Cambridge, MA: Harvard University Press, 1992).

7. This attitude is not as present among the Lubavitchers, who believe in embracing all Jews, no matter what their level of observance.

8. The 1960s saw an influx of blacks and Latinos into Williamsburg, and a similar migration of blacks into Crown Heights. See Egon Mayer, *From Suburb to Shtetl: The Jews of Boro Park* (Philadelphia: Temple University Press, 1979).

9. The Lubavitch rebbe made a point of keeping his court in Crown Heights, which remains today the headquarters of the Lubavitch movement. The Satmar rebbe also remained in Williamsburg, although many Satmar Hasidim did make the move to Boro Park.

10. See Egon Mayer, *From Suburb to Shtetl.*

Chapter Two

1. My knowledge of this comes not only from interviews, but from my experience attending a modesty lecture for women, given in a Hasidic community in Brooklyn.

2. In addition to going to the mikvah, the other positive commandments a woman must perform are: lighting Sabbath candles and separating and burning a piece of challah that is baked for the Sabbath.

Chapter Three

1. Statistics on Hasidic poverty are hard to come by. For some information on this subject, see Joe Sexton, "When Work Is Not Enough: Religion and Welfare Shape Economics for the Hasidim," *New York Times*, April 21, 1997. According to Sexton, one-third of the estimated seven thousand families in Hasidic Williamsburg are on public assistance. According to the 2000 Census, 61.7 percent of the families in the upstate New York Satmar enclave of Kiryas Joel were living below the poverty line (U.S. Bureau of the Census).

2. See Ada Rapoport-Albert, ed., *Hasidism Reappraised* (Portland: Valentine Mitchell & Co., 1996).

3. See Jerome R. Mintz, *Hasidic People: A Place in the New World* (Cambridge, MA: Harvard University Press, 1992).

4. See Janet Belcove-Shalin, , ed., *New World Hasidim: Ethnographic Studies of Hasidic Jews in America* (Albany: SUNY Press, 1995), p. 9.

5. George Kranzler, *Hasidic Williamsburg: A Contemporary American Hasidic Community* (Northvale, NJ: Jason Aronson, 1995).

6. Even today, many non-Hasidic Jews believe that the Lubavitchers who consider their late rebbe to be the Messiah are engaging in idol worship. See David Berger, *The Rebbe, the Messiah, and the Scandal of Orthodox Indifference* (London: Littman Library of Jewish Civilization, 2001).

7. Members of Hasidic communities tend to vote in local, state, and federal elections for those endorsed by their leaders.

Chapter Four

1. See Nacha Cattan, "Orthodox Rehab Programs: Too Much of a Good Thing," *The Forward*, August 17, 2001, and Michele Chabin, "On Their Own and Using Drugs," *The Jewish Week*, January 28, 2005.

2. See Stewart Ain, "Teen Crisis Detailed in Orthodox Brooklyn," *New York Magazine* (December 20, 1999).

3. Ibid.

4. In Jewish law, the crime of adultery can be committed technically only by and with a married woman. This is related to the fact that, according to the Torah, a man may have more than one wife while a woman has one husband, and to the idea that a woman can build only one home. This is not to suggest that extramarital relations are condoned among men in the Hasidic world.

Chapter Six

1. Among the Hasidim, "ultra-Orthodox" is considered a misnomer, and, to some, a pejorative term. To these Jews there is nothing "ultra" or extreme about their observance. Some prefer to refer to themselves as "strictly Orthodox," or "Torah true" Jews. In Israel the preferred term is "haredi."

2. Menachem Mendel Schneerson.

3. Chabad is an acronym for the Hebrew words *chochma* (wisdom), *bina* (understanding), and *daas* (knowledge).

4. That is, their heritage according to Lubavitch, which originated in Eastern Europe and reflects Ashkenazi Jewish traditions.

5. There is a long history of antagonism between Satmar and Lubavitch. For more information on this, see Ari L. Goldman, "Attack on Rabbi Brings Anguish to Boro Park," *New York Times*, June 23, 1983.

6. A survey on Orthodox Jewish women's sexuality conducted by Dr. Rachel Yehuda and Dr. Michelle Friedman found that 15.7 percent of Jewish women claimed to have experienced sexual abuse before the age of thirteen, and 9.9 percent after age thirteen. These numbers were not much different

from those of the larger survey of American women, which revealed that 17.2 percent experienced sexual abuse before the age of thirteen, and 9.2 percent after thirteen. See "Survey Released on Jewish Women's Sexuality," *The Forward*, May 7, 2004.

7. See David Rose, "Jewish Code of Silence Hushes Scandals," *The Observer*, August 4, 1991, p. 6.

8. This is not to suggest, however, that other groups do not engage in cover-ups over sexually abusive behavior. One need only look at the recent revelations concerning the Catholic Church and the military to see that this approach is in no way limited to the Jews.

9. Only men are allowed to put on tefillin, while it is the woman's responsibility to light the Shabbos candles.

Chapter Seven

1. See Greg B. Smith in the *New York Daily News*, January 26, 2001, pg. 3.

Chapter Eight

1. See Michele Chabin, "On Their Own and Using Drugs," *The Jewish Week*, January 28, 2005.

Chapter Nine

1. For more on this, see Alan Dundes, *The Shabbat Elevator and Other Sabbath Subterfuges* (Lanham, MD: Rowman and Littlefield, 2002).